POSTAL

EXAM STUDY GUIDE

Ace your USPS VEA 955 - 474 - 475 - 477 on the First Try | Tests, Q&A, Audio, Extra Content

Talon Redwood

EXAM STUDY GUIDE

TABLE OF CONTENTS

INTRODUCTION

The Postal Service, for generations, has played a pivotal role in shaping the course of communication across the nation. Its historical importance is intertwined with the tapestry of stories and achievements of countless individuals who have dedicated themselves to connecting people, no matter the distance. The heartbeat of this intricate system is powered by its dedicated workforce, and entering its ranks is no small task. For aspirants aiming to embark on this rewarding journey, the Postal Exam is the critical first step.

Deeply rooted in the traditions of the American communication infrastructure, the Postal Exam is more than just a series of tests. It symbolizes the commitment to excellence, punctuality, and reliability that the Postal Service values in its employees. The exam assesses the candidate's aptitude and readiness for the challenges ahead and tests their dedication to upholding the esteemed values of the service.

While the foundation of the Postal Service remains unshakeable, the world around it is constantly evolving. Technological advancements, ever-changing customer demands, and emerging global challenges necessitate the Postal Service to innovate and adapt continually. Correspondingly, the Postal Exam has evolved over the years to ensure it remains reflective of the current needs and demands of the service.

This guide aims to provide a comprehensive overview of the modern-day Postal Exam while nodding to its storied past. Navigating the complexities of the Postal Exam without adequate preparation is akin to setting out on a journey without a map. While natural aptitude and common sense are undoubtedly valuable, the nuances of the exam demand a deeper understanding and a structured approach to study.

Moreover, with the sheer number of aspirants competing for a limited number of positions, the margin for error is fragile. A dedicated preparation regimen, therefore, elevates your chances of success and instills confidence, reducing exam-day jitters.

One might question the relevance of medical terminologies in a postal exam guide. The answer lies in understanding the multi-faceted nature of postal duties. Since many postal roles involve physically demanding tasks, a basic understanding of medical terms can be beneficial. T

hese terminologies play a subtle yet significant role, whether it's discerning between different types of strains or injuries, recognizing signs of fatigue, or understanding ergonomic principles to ensure safety during heavy lifting.

At first glance, the Postal Exam might seem daunting. It's a tapestry of various sections, each designed to probe specific competence areas. Some segments focus on memory and attention to detail, while others test problem-solving abilities. These varied sections are meticulously crafted to ascertain that those who pass are cut out for the intricate tasks the Postal Service demands.

This guide is structured to be your trusted companion in this journey. By walking you through each section, offering insights into the nature of questions, and providing tips and strategies, we aim to make the seemingly arduous journey of Postal Exam preparation smoother and more manageable.

The Postal Service embodies tradition, reliability, and innovation, and entering its esteemed ranks is both an honor and a responsibility. By choosing to embark on this path, you're not just aiming for a job but becoming part of a legacy. The Postal Exam is your gateway, and this guide is crafted with the singular purpose of helping you cross that threshold with confidence.

As we delve deeper into the subsequent chapters, let's remember the weight of the responsibility of being a part of the Postal Service. It's not just about delivering mail; it's about connecting lives, bridging distances, and being the silent custodians of countless stories, hopes, and dreams. So, here's to a journey of learning, preparation, and eventual success. Welcome to the world of the Postal Exam.

BRIEF DESCRIPTION

When we peel back the layers of history, we find that the Postal Service has been a cornerstone of America's growth and development. From the initial horseback riders traversing rugged terrains to today's state-of-the-art systems, it's a legacy built on trust, efficiency, and tenacity. And the gatekeepers to this legacy? The Postal Exams.

At its core, the Postal Exam seeks to identify individuals who not only have the technical know-how but also the intrinsic qualities necessary to uphold the high standards of the Postal Service. Think of it as a beacon, casting its light to find those with the resilience, aptitude, and dedication to serve communities nationwide.

Now, why are these exams so detailed and intricate? To understand that, we must first grasp the multi-faceted roles within the Postal Service. These range from processing vast amounts of mail with pinpoint accuracy to the physical demands of delivery, often braving the elements. Every task in the Postal Service is a cog in a much larger machine. And for this machine to run seamlessly, each cog needs to function flawlessly.

Beyond the evident physical demands, there's a lesser-discussed angle to postal duties: understanding basic medical terminologies. On the surface, it might appear incongruous. Why would a mail carrier need to be versed in medical jargon?

The answer lies in the everyday challenges these professionals face. Discerning the initial symptoms of heatstroke on a sweltering summer day or understanding the ergonomic implications of lifting heavy packages—having a foundational grasp of medical terms can be the difference between routine operations and avoidable mishaps.

The Postal Exams are not a monolithic entity but a spectrum of assessments, each tailored for specific roles within the service. These exams delve deep, probing various aspects of a candidate's abilities. These exams leave no stone unturned, from memory tests that challenge one's retention capabilities to logical reasoning sections that evaluate problem-solving skills.

For instance, imagine the task of sorting mail. It's not just about identifying destinations but doing so with impeccable speed and accuracy, all while adhering to safety protocols. Such a task necessitates a sharp memory, attention to detail, and understanding of specific medical precautions. The exams, therefore, are structured to ascertain these very competencies.

Why place such emphasis on these exams? Simply put, the Postal Service is the silent backbone of America's communication infrastructure. Any glitches, delays, or misplacements can ripple out, affecting countless lives. Hence, the importance of ensuring that every recruit is not just good but exceptional.

Moreover, with technological advancements, the role of the Postal Service has become even more nuanced. In today's digital age, while many communications have moved online, the value of tangible mail still needs to be improved. Whether it's crucial medical supplies, legal documents, or cherished personal letters, the Postal Service handles items that often carry significant emotional or practical importance. Thus, the Postal Exams ensure that those entrusted with these responsibilities are the best fit. Beyond the operational efficiency of the Postal Service, these exams play a more profound role. They underscore the service's commitment to excellence. When a resident sees their mail carrier braving a snowstorm or a downpour, it's not just about delivering a package. It's a testament to the dedication, resilience, and commitment that the Postal Exam identifies and nurtures.

Ultimately, the Postal Exams are not just about assessing competencies; they're about continuing a legacy built on trust. For the countless individuals waiting for that college acceptance letter, that critical medical report, or that cherished note from a loved one, the Postal Service represents hope, joy, and connection. Ensuring that this legacy thrives and grows, one delivery at a time, is the profound importance of the Postal Exams.

As we navigate through the subsequent sections of this guide, it's vital to remember that preparing for the Postal Exam is not just about securing a job. It's about embracing a role that impacts communities, connects lives, and upholds a tradition that has been the bedrock of American communication. It's a journey worth embarking upon, with the Postal Exam as the first significant milestone

GENERAL ELIGIBILITY AND REQUIREMENTS

Embarking on a career with the Postal Service is not just a matter of acing the Postal Exam. Before even approaching the starting line, aspirants must meet a series of eligibility criteria and requirements. These stipulations ensure that the Postal Service maintains its esteemed standards and continues to operate with the same dedication, efficiency, and reliability expected by the nation. Let's delve deeper into what these general eligibility and requirements entail.

At its core, the eligibility criteria are not just checkboxes to tick off but a reflection of the Postal Service's commitment to excellence. The Service operates on the premise that every member, irrespective of their role, plays an integral part in upholding its reputation. Therefore, these requirements are designed to identify individuals who align with the service's ethos and are equipped to handle the job's multi-faceted challenges.

One of the fundamental requirements is the age stipulation. Aspirants seeking the Postal Service must have attained a certain age threshold. This requirement ensures that candidates possess a maturity level suitable for the role's responsibilities. In this context, age is more than just a number; it represents an individual's life experiences, judgment capabilities, and potential resilience in high-pressure situations.

While the Postal Service is an inclusive employer, there's an undeniable emphasis on educational qualifications. A certain foundational academic level ensures that candidates possess the necessary cognitive skills and are committed to learning and personal development. Specialized training might also be a prerequisite in specific roles where detailed technical knowledge becomes paramount. This specialized training, especially when intertwined with medical terminologies, ensures that postal workers can understand and address any health-related concerns that might arise during their duties.

Given the nature of many roles within the Postal Service, there's a spotlight on physical fitness. Candidates must often meet specific physical criteria reflective of the job's demands. Whether it's lifting heavy packages, walking long distances, or withstanding extreme weather conditions, the service needs to ensure that its employees are physically equipped to handle the rigors of the job. From a medical perspective, understanding one's physical limitations and capacities can be crucial in ensuring personal safety and operational efficiency. The trustworthiness and reliability of the Postal Service are built on the integrity of its employees. Given the sensitive nature of many shipments—personal letters, legal documents, or medical supplies—a rigorous background check is non-negotiable. Aspirants must demonstrate a history free from any activities that could compromise the integrity of the service. Further security clearances might also be necessary for roles that involve handling susceptible material.

Beyond the tangible criteria, the Postal Service places immense value on specific personal attributes. Attributes such as reliability, punctuality, and an unwavering commitment to service excellence are highly sought after. Soft skills, including communication abilities, problem-solving prowess, and teamwork, are equally critical. In many ways, these attributes bridge the technical aspects of the job and the human connections that the Postal Service cherishes.

In today's rapidly evolving landscape, adaptability and a commitment to continual learning are more than desirable traits—they're essential. The Postal Service constantly innovates, adopting new technologies and refining its processes. As a result, aspirants must demonstrate a willingness and aptitude for continuous learning, ensuring they remain abreast of the latest developments and can seamlessly integrate them into their roles.

While the eligibility criteria and requirements might appear stringent at first glance, they underscore the Postal Service's commitment to maintaining its gold standard of operations. For aspirants, meeting these requirements is more than just a hurdle. It's a testament to their dedication, resilience, and alignment with the core values of the service.

As we navigate the intricacies of the Postal Service's eligibility maze, we must view each criterion not as a barrier but as a stepping stone toward a rewarding career. A career that is not just about delivering packages but about upholding a legacy, connecting communities, and being at the forefront of America's communication backbone.

STUDY MATERIAL AND PREPARATION

The journey to joining the Postal Service is not just about meeting eligibility criteria; it's about proving one's aptitude, skills, and dedication through rigorous examinations. Like any significant endeavor, success in the Postal Exams requires meticulous preparation, and having suitable study material is paramount. Equipped with the correct resources, candidates can confidently navigate the challenges of these exams, ensuring they not only pass but excel.

EXAM 955 - MAINTENANCE AND ELECTRONICS

Diving into the various Postal Exams, Exam 955, focusing on Maintenance and Electronics, stands out as a distinctive assessment tailored for specific roles within the Postal Service. As we peel back the layers of this exam, aspirants will uncover the nuances, intricacies, and challenges inherent to it. Preparing for Exam 955 demands more than just a superficial understanding; it necessitates a deep dive into maintenance protocols and the world of electronics.

A Fusion of Domains: Exam 955 represents a fusion of two pivotal domains: maintenance and electronics. It's a testament to the evolving landscape of the Postal Service, where technological advancement meets operational efficiency. The Postal Service, though steeped in tradition, has continually adapted to the changing times, incorporating cutting-edge technologies to ensure seamless operations. This integration is reflected in Exam 955.

Deciphering Maintenance: Maintenance, in the context of the Postal Service, is not just about fixing what's broken. It's about preventive measures, understanding the intricate machinery, and ensuring that operations run without a hitch. From sorting machines that process thousands of letters per hour to conveyor systems that transport packages, the machinery's health is pivotal.

Candidates preparing for Exam 955 must familiarize themselves with the various machinery types, components, and operational intricacies. Understanding the medical implications, such as ergonomic principles that guide safe machinery operation or recognizing the initial symptoms of overexertion, can be crucial. This knowledge ensures that maintenance personnel can work efficiently while safeguarding their well-being.

The World of Electronics: Electronics, as addressed in Exam 955, delves into the heart of the machinery. It's not just about wires and circuits but understanding how these components form complex systems. In the age of digitalization, even the most traditional machines in the Postal Service have electronic components that ensure precision and efficiency.

Preparation in this domain requires candidates to have a solid foundational understanding of electronic principles. Concepts such as circuit design, signal processing, and even basic programming might come into play. Given the convergence of technology and health, knowledge about how electronic components might interact with medical devices, such as pacemakers or hearing aids, can also be crucial.

A Comprehensive Approach: Candidates should approach Exam 955 not as two separate entities but as a cohesive whole. It's about understanding how maintenance protocols complement electronic components and vice versa. Preparation, therefore, should be holistic. Engaging with hands-on training, leveraging simulation tools, and understanding real-world scenarios can be immensely beneficial.

Utilizing Resources. Given the specialized nature of Exam 955, relying on generic study material won't suffice. Candidates should seek resources specifically tailored for this exam. Engaging with Postal Service veterans, joining dedicated study groups, and exploring online forums can provide insights that traditional textbooks might miss.

Practice Makes Perfect: Finally, as with any exam, practice is pivotal. Regularly taking mock tests, timing oneself, and understanding the exam pattern can make the difference between passing and excelling. As candidates navigate the world of Exam 955, it's essential to remember that every challenge encountered is a stepping stone, a learning opportunity, pushing them closer to their goal.

Exam 955, with its dual focus on maintenance and electronics, represents the new age of the Postal Service—a blend of tradition and technology. Approached with dedication, curiosity, and the right resources, candidates can ensure they're prepared and poised for success.

BASIC ELECTRONICS: UNDERSTANDING CIRCUITS, COMPONENTS, AND TOOLS

In the intricate web of postal operations, the underpinnings of modern machinery lie deeply entrenched in electronics. At the heart of this realm is the science of circuits, components, and the tools that bring them to life. To master Exam 955, one cannot merely skim the surface of electronics; a profound grasp of these fundamental concepts is indispensable.

The Symphony of Circuits: To understand electronics is to immerse oneself in the world of circuits. A circuit is a closed path through which electric current flows. Think of it as a highway system for electrons, where traffic flow is meticulously orchestrated to ensure functionality and efficiency. While circuits can range from simple to staggeringly complex, they all adhere to foundational principles that dictate their behavior.

When we address circuits, Ohm's Law invariably emerges as a cornerstone concept. It relates the circuit's voltage, current, and resistance, providing a mathematical representation of their relationship. Grasping Ohm's Law paves the way for a deeper appreciation of how circuits function and how their components interact.

Components: The Building Blocks: In the vast electronics ecosystem, components are akin to the individual organisms that form an intricate ecosystem. Each has a unique role, and their collective interplay determines the health and functionality of the entire system.

1. **Resistors:** Often considered the gatekeepers of a circuit, resistors regulate the current flow. Just as a valve might control the water flow in a pipe, a resistor manages the passage of electrons, ensuring that other components receive the appropriate amount of current.

2. **Capacitors:** These are the storage units of the electronic world. Capacitors store and release energy as needed, much like a dam holds and releases water. Their role becomes pivotal in regulating voltage and ensuring it remains stable across a circuit.

3. **Transistors:** Acting as the switchboard operators of a circuit, transistors can amplify or switch electronic signals, directing traffic and ensuring that signals reach their intended destinations.

4. **Diodes:** These one-way streets of the electronic world allow current to flow in only one direction. This unidirectional flow is essential in converting alternating current (AC) to direct current (DC).

From a health standpoint, understanding these components is crucial. For instance, if malfunctioning, capacitors can release stored energy abruptly, posing potential hazards. A thorough understanding ensures that postal workers can safely interact with electronic systems and recognize early signs of component failure.

Tools of the Trade

In the electronics orchestra, if circuits and components are the musicians, then tools are the conductors, ensuring harmony and precision. Acquainting yourself with these tools is non-negotiable for anyone delving deep into electronics.

1. **Multimeters:** These versatile devices measure voltage, current, and resistance, offering a comprehensive glimpse into a circuit's health. Learning to use a multimeter proficiently is akin to a doctor mastering the stethoscope—it becomes an extension of one's senses.

2. **Oscilloscopes:** For those keen on visual insights, oscilloscopes graphically display electrical signals, allowing technicians to visualize fluctuations in voltage over time. This is essential for troubleshooting and understanding complex waveforms.

3. **Soldering Irons:** Soldering irons come into play when components need to be securely attached to a circuit board. Mastery over soldering ensures solid connections, minimizing the risk of malfunction.

4. **Logic Analyzers:** Understanding the sequence of high and low signals is paramount in digital circuits. Logic analyzers, in this context, provide a chronological view of these signals, aiding in diagnostics and rectification.

Cultivating a Holistic Perspective

While understanding circuits, components, and tools is foundational, true mastery lies in cultivating a holistic perspective; it's about recognizing the interplay, the dance of electrons, and the harmonious synergy of components. Electronics, especially in the context of the Postal Service, is not an isolated domain but an integral cog in a grand machine.

By weaving together knowledge, curiosity, and hands-on experience, aspirants can ensure they're prepared and genuinely attuned to the pulse of electronics, ready to ace Exam 955 and embark on a fulfilling journey in the Postal Service.

Safety Procedures: Best Practices for Safe Work in Electrical and Mechanical Environments

Working in electrical and mechanical domains is not just about skill and precision; it's about maintaining an environment where safety reigns supreme. The delicate dance of electrons and the robustness of machinery can present hazards if approached without caution.

For those delving into the world of the Postal Service, where electronics and mechanics converge, understanding and implementing safety procedures is paramount. Ensuring safety is not merely a protocol—it's a mindset that safeguards the machinery and every individual working in proximity.

The Essence of Electrical Safety

Electrical environments pulsate with energy. From circuits buzzing with currents to machines powered by electricity, the omnipresence of electrical energy is both a marvel and a potential hazard.

1. **Understanding Circuit Behavior:** At the heart of electrical safety is a thorough grasp of circuits' behavior. Recognizing the nuances of voltage, current, and resistance and how they interplay can preempt many hazards. For instance, understanding that water is a conductor can avert potential short circuits or electrocution risks.

2. **Grounding and Insulation:** These are the sentinels of electrical safety. Grounding ensures that any unintended electrical surge has a safe pathway, minimizing the risk of shocks. Insulation is a protective barrier, preventing unintentional contact with electrical components.

3. **Safe Distancing:** Maintaining a safe distance is crucial when working with high-voltage machinery or circuits. Even proximity to high-voltage areas can lead to arcing, where electricity can "jump," posing risks.

4. **Using Protective Gear:** Just as a physician don gloves and a mask, those working in electrical environments should equip themselves with safety gloves, insulated tools, and eye protection. These aren't just accessories; they're shields against potential hazards.

Mechanical Safety: The Dance of Machinery

With its moving parts and robust operations, a machine can be both mesmerizing and intimidating. Mechanical safety is about recognizing the power of these machines and ensuring that this power doesn't become a peril.

1. **Regular Maintenance:** At the core of mechanical safety is ensuring that machinery is in optimal health. Regular maintenance checks, from oiling moving parts to ensuring that gears are aligned, can prevent sudden malfunctions, which might lead to accidents.

2. **Understanding Machine Operations:** Before operating any machinery, one must be familiar with its functions. Only thinking of operating levers or switches without comprehending their implications can be a recipe for disaster.

3. **Emergency Stops:** Every piece of machinery should have easily accessible emergency stops. In situations where something goes awry, being able to halt operations instantly can be a lifesaver.

4. **Avoiding Loose Clothing and Hair:** Machines can easily catch loose hair or clothing in a mechanical environment. Ensuring hair is tied back and avoiding flowing garments can prevent entanglement hazards.

Intertwining Safety Protocols

Safety procedures should be intertwined in environments where electrical and mechanical realms converge. It's about understanding that an electrical malfunction can have mechanical implications and vice versa.

1. **Regular Training:** Safety isn't a one-time lesson but an ongoing education. Regular training sessions, safety drills, and workshops can keep safety protocols fresh in memory, ensuring that they're instinctively followed.

2. **First Aid and Medical Preparedness:** Despite all precautions, accidents can happen. Being prepared for such eventualities is crucial. Having a well-equipped first aid kit and trained personnel can mitigate the impact of any accident. Understanding medical implications, like how electrical shocks affect cardiac rhythms, can guide immediate interventions.

3. **Clear Signage:** Both electrical and mechanical environments should have clear signage indicating potential hazards, emergency exits, and safety equipment locations. This visual guidance can be instrumental in both preventing accidents and navigating emergencies.

In the grand tapestry of the Postal Service operations, where machinery and electronics are the threads weaving intricate patterns, safety procedures are the knots that ensure the tapestry remains intact and beautiful. For every aspirant keen on diving into this world, imbibing these safety protocols is not just a responsibility but a pledge to safeguard oneself, colleagues, and the essence of the Postal Service.

Building Maintenance: Plumbing, Carpentry, and Other Related Topics

Maintenance tasks, while less technologically intense than electronics, form the backbone of any facility's operations, especially within the vast expanse of the Postal Service. Understanding the facets of building maintenance - from plumbing to carpentry - is essential for anyone tasked with keeping a facility running smoothly. A comprehensive grasp of these domains ensures that the structural and functional integrity of the infrastructure remains uncompromised.

Plumbing: The Veins of a Facility

Much like the circulatory system in our bodies, plumbing systems transport essential resources - water, in this case - to various parts of a building. Ensuring this system's efficiency and health is paramount.

1. **Pipe Anatomy:** At the core of any plumbing system lies its network of pipes. Understanding the materials (like PVC, copper, or PEX), their appropriate usage and their vulnerabilities help in installations and diagnostics.

2. **Valves and Faucets:** These control water flow, acting as gatekeepers. Being acquainted with different types of valves, from ball to gate valves, allows for precision in control and repair.

3. **Drainage and Waste Systems:** A robust plumbing system efficiently removes wastewater beyond supply. Grasping the intricacies of traps, vents, and waste lines ensures that waste exits without causing blockages or backflows.

4. **Water Heating:** Whether for comfort or specific functionalities, understanding water heaters, their types, and maintenance procedures is essential. Recognizing common issues, such as sediment buildup or thermostat malfunctions, ensures consistent supply.

Carpentry: Crafting and Mending Structures

Carpentry, with its confluence of art and science, plays a pivotal role in creating and maintaining a building's structural elements.

1. **Types of Wood:** Every task in carpentry begins with selecting the appropriate wood. Understanding the strengths, vulnerabilities, and best-use scenarios for woods like oak, pine, or mahogany can define the longevity of any project.

2. **Joinery Techniques:** How wood pieces connect determines the strength of the structure. Familiarizing oneself with techniques like dovetailing, mortise, tenon, or biscuit joining provides versatility in crafting.

3. **Use of Tools:** Mastery in carpentry is as much about skill as it is about using the right tools. Knowing their functionalities and safety procedures is essential, whether it's a chisel, a plane, or a power saw.

4. **Finishings and Protection:** Once structures are in place, protecting them against wear, tear, and environmental factors becomes paramount. Understanding varnishes, sealants, and paint types ensures that wooden frames remain pristine.

Masonry and Tiling

The foundation of many buildings, masonry work, and tiling provide aesthetic appeal and structural robustness.

1. **Types of Bricks and Stones:** From cinder blocks to limestone or marble, understanding the various materials, their strengths, and their aesthetic appeal can guide construction and maintenance tasks.

2. **Mortars and Adhesives:** Binding materials together requires the right mix of substances. Whether choosing the right mortar mix for brickwork or the appropriate adhesive for tiles, this knowledge can determine the longevity of structures.

3. **Tiling Patterns and Maintenance:** Beyond mere installation, understanding how tiles can be patterned for visual appeal and how they can be maintained, especially in high-traffic areas, is essential.

HVAC (Heating, Ventilation, and Air Conditioning)

Ensuring the comfort of a facility's inhabitants and the optimal equipment functioning often hinges on the HVAC system's efficiency.

1. **Types of Systems:** From centralized systems to split units, recognizing the functionalities, advantages, and limitations of various HVAC systems can guide installation, usage, and repair decisions.

2. **Air Quality Management:** HVAC is not just about temperature control. Ensuring that air quality, including parameters like humidity and pollutant levels, remains within healthy ranges is crucial.

3. **Maintenance and Diagnostics:** Regular check-ups, understanding common issues like refrigerant leaks or duct blockages, and conducting timely repairs ensure the HVAC system's longevity.

Painting and Finishing

The final touches to any maintenance task often involve painting and finishing, which, while enhancing aesthetics, also offer protection.

1. **Types of Paint:** From oil-based paints to latex ones, choosing the right paint type can affect longevity, finish, and drying time.

2. **Surface Preparation:** Before any paint touches a surface, ensuring that the surface is clean, primed, and suitable for painting is crucial.

3. **Protective Finishes:** Beyond aesthetics, finishes like sealants or weatherproofing agents can provide added protection against environmental factors.

In conclusion, building maintenance is a vast domain, intricately woven with multiple disciplines. A holistic understanding is imperative for anyone stepping into this realm, especially within the Postal Service's context. It's about recognizing that every screw turned, every pipe fixed, and every beam crafted contributes to the larger tapestry of efficient operations. Maintenance is not just about mending; it's about ensuring that the facility, in all its complexity, stands as a testament to resilience, efficiency, and excellence.

Schematics & Electrical Diagrams: Reading and Interpreting

In electrical and electronic systems, schematics and electrical diagrams serve as the primary language of communication. These intricate illustrations and symbols offer a snapshot of how systems function, interconnect, and can be diagnosed or repaired.

For maintenance professionals, mainly within vast establishments like the Postal Service, being adept at reading and interpreting these diagrams is paramount. This not only streamlines troubleshooting but also ensures safety and efficiency in operations.

At its core, a schematic diagram represents the relationships and connections between different electronic or electrical system components. Unlike pictorial diagrams, which might display components as they physically appear, schematics focus on the electrical connections, fostering a deeper understanding of the system's workings.

When encountering a schematic, one must appreciate its layered nature. These diagrams don't merely illustrate; they narrate a story of electrons, their pathways, and their interactions with various components.

Basic Symbols and Their Interpretations

Every language has its alphabet, and it's the myriad symbols for electrical schematics. Recognizing them is the first step to fluency.

- **Resistors:** Often depicted as a zig-zag line, resistors are pivotal in controlling current flow. They ensure that components receive the appropriate amount of current, preventing potential damage.

- **Capacitors:** These are usually represented as two parallel lines. Capacitors store energy and can influence the timing of electronic events.

- **Diodes:** A-line and triangle combined represent diodes. These components ensure that the current flows in only one direction, offering protection to circuits.

- **Transistors:** Comprising two diode-like symbols, transistors act as amplifiers or switches in many circuits.

- **Switches:** Simple break-lines or angled lines represent switches that control the current flow by either closing (completing) or opening (interrupting) a circuit.

By understanding the meaning behind these symbols, one sees the schematic as a vibrant, animated landscape rather than a static picture.

Tracing Pathways and Understanding Flow

With a basic understanding of symbols, the next challenge is to trace the current flow. Remember, electrons naturally move from regions of high potential to low potential. This flow, often indicated by arrows or implied by the arrangement of components, becomes the central theme of any schematic.

Tracing these pathways can deduce how a system reacts when powered, which components play pivotal roles, and where potential issues might arise.

Interpreting Advanced Symbols and Concepts

Beyond the basics, schematics can become intricate, featuring symbols or notations that depict advanced components or concepts.

- **Relays and Solenoids:** These electromagnetic devices, usually represented by a coil symbol, act as switches controlled by electrical power. They play crucial roles in many automation processes.

- **Integrated Circuits (ICs):** Represented as a box with multiple leads, ICs are complex assemblies that might have thousands of components within. They often come with their own mini-schematics or pin-out diagrams.

- **Ground Connections:** These are crucial for the safety and functioning of circuits. Symbols, like three descending horizontal lines, indicate these connections.

Importance of Color Codes and Annotations

Many schematics employ color codes or annotations to add layers of information. For instance, different wire colors might indicate different voltage levels or functions. Conversely, annotations can provide specifics about component values, model numbers, or other vital data.

Utilizing Schematics in Diagnostics

When systems falter, schematics become invaluable. They allow professionals to pinpoint areas that might be malfunctioning, recommend replacements, or understand how modifications can influence performance. For instance, if a specific component like a resistor keeps failing, referring to the schematic can reveal if it's exposed to higher currents than intended.

Safety and Precautions

While schematics provide knowledge, it's essential to couple this with safety. Always ensure that circuits are powered down, and capacitors are discharged when working on them. Misinterpretations can lead to dangerous situations, so always double-check and refer to annotations or supplementary guides when unsure.

To the uninitiated, schematics might appear as mere doodles. However, for those in the know, they unfold as intricate tales of electrons dancing through pathways, components working in harmony, and systems achieving their intended functions.

For maintenance professionals in establishments as pivotal as the Postal Service, mastering the art of reading and interpreting these diagrams becomes not just a skill but a necessity. It bridges the gap between abstract concepts and real-world applications, ensuring that the vast communication machinery operates seamlessly, safely, and efficiently.

Troubleshooting & Repair: Identifying and Fixing Common Issues

Maintenance plays a critical part in the demanding landscape of postal services, where timely deliveries and smooth operations become the backbone of daily functions. Among the varied responsibilities of these roles, troubleshooting and repair stand out as pivotal.

When equipment or systems falter, professionals must promptly identify issues and restore functionality. This section delves into the essential techniques and methods for efficient troubleshooting and repair.

Embracing a Systematic Approach

Troubleshooting isn't about random guesswork; it's a structured, step-by-step process that identifies problems, determines their root causes, and offers solutions. To diagnose effectively, one needs to approach situations methodically.

- **Observation:** Begin by keenly observing the equipment or system. Often, issues manifest visually - unusual lights, atypical sounds, or erratic movements. These observations can hint at where the problems lie.

- **Documentation:** Before diving deep, always refer to the equipment's manuals, schematics, or any maintenance logs. Past issues or manufacturer's guidelines can give insights into potential problem areas.

- **Isolation:** If a system consists of multiple parts or circuits, try isolating them individually. This tactic narrows down the problematic area, making it easier to diagnose and subsequently repair.

Embracing Advanced Diagnostic Tools

In today's technologically advanced era, various diagnostic tools have emerged that streamline the troubleshooting process. Utilizing these tools not only speeds up the identification of problems but also enhances accuracy.

- **Multimeters:** These devices measure voltage, current, and resistance. They are indispensable in detecting whether electrical components are functioning as they should.

- **Oscilloscopes:** For more complex electrical issues, especially in circuits with fluctuating signals, an oscilloscope provides a visual representation of electrical waveforms, allowing technicians to pinpoint irregularities.

- **Thermal Imaging Cameras:** Heat can be a sign of malfunction. With thermal cameras, professionals can detect areas of excessive heat, often indicating issues like short circuits or worn-out components.

Understanding Common Issues and Their Resolutions

While each piece of equipment or system is unique, specific common issues plague many electrical and mechanical setups. Recognizing these often expedites the troubleshooting process.

- **Loose Connections:** Vibrations, wear and tear, or subpar installations can lead to loose connections. Regularly inspecting and ensuring tight harmonies can preempt many potential issues.

- **Worn-Out Components:** Components, especially moving ones, wear out over time. Bearings might become noisy, belts may slip, and electrical components could burn out. Regular maintenance checks and timely replacements ensure longevity.

- **Software Glitches:** In the digital age, software governs many systems. Sometimes, malfunctions stem from software bugs or glitches. Simple resets or software updates often rectify such issues.

- **Environmental Factors:** Humidity, temperature fluctuations, or dust can influence equipment performance. Ensure that systems operate within their recommended ecological conditions.

Safety First: Ensuring Safe Repair Practices

While efficiency is vital, safety remains paramount. Before diving into repairs, always:

- **Disconnect Power:** Before working on any electrical system, disconnect its power source. This precaution prevents accidental electrocutions.

- **Use Personal Protective Equipment (PPE):** Depending on the work environment, using gloves, safety glasses, or even ear protection can safeguard against potential injuries.

- **Stay Informed:** Always be aware of high-voltage areas or components that store energy, like capacitors. A well-informed technician is a safe technician.

Post-repair Checks: Ensuring Functionality

After repairs, it's crucial to take time to get systems back into operation. Conduct thorough post-repair checks to ensure everything functions as intended. Test the equipment under different conditions and monitor for any irregularities.

Keeping Abreast with Technological Advancements

The maintenance world is ever-evolving, with new technologies and techniques emerging regularly. To remain effective in troubleshooting and repair, professionals must continually upgrade their knowledge. This might involve attending workshops, undergoing additional training, or engaging in online forums and communities.

Even minor hiccups can cascade into significant operational challenges in the vast machinery of postal services. Hence, efficient troubleshooting and repair are not just maintenance tasks but crucial cogs in ensuring seamless service delivery.

By approaching problems systematically, utilizing advanced tools, understanding common issues, prioritizing safety, and staying updated, professionals can ensure they're always prepared to tackle challenges, keeping the wheels of the postal service turning smoothly.

EXAM 474 - MAIL CARRIER VEA

Delivering mail is more than just carrying letters from one place to another. It's committed to ensuring that vital information, precious sentiments, and crucial documents reach their intended recipients on time and in pristine condition. As one of the most iconic figures representing the U.S. Postal Service, a mail carrier holds a position of trust, responsibility, and dedication.

Ensuring the selection of the most competent individuals for this role is the purpose of Exam 474, also known as the Mail Carrier VEA (Virtual Entry Assessment). Let's journey into an in-depth exploration of this pivotal examination.

Unraveling the Essence of Exam 474

At its core, Exam 474 assesses the potential and proficiency of candidates aspiring to join the ranks of mail carriers. Unlike other jobs, a mail carrier interacts with the public daily, faces numerous logistical challenges, and must handle the immense responsibility of managing sensitive material. The VEA ensures that candidates possess the essential skills, temperament, and knowledge to excel in this demanding role.

A Dive into the Test Format

Exam 474 is a digital assessment emphasizing the modern shift of the U.S. Postal Service towards leveraging technology in its operations. Candidates typically take the test online, which allows for a streamlined evaluation process and swift feedback.

The assessment encompasses a variety of sections, each honing in on specific skills and attributes crucial for a mail carrier:

- **Personal Characteristics and Experience Inventory:** This segment dives into a candidate's past experiences and evaluates personality traits. Given the public-facing nature of the job, mail carriers need to exhibit patience, empathy, and practical interpersonal skills. This section paints a comprehensive picture of a candidate's behavioral tendencies and potential fit for the role through a series of scenario-based questions.

- **Task-Based Simulations:** A mail carrier's day is punctuated by multiple tasks - from sorting mail and identifying the fastest routes to managing undeliverable items and facing inclement weather. This section immerses candidates in virtual simulations of typical challenges, gauging their problem-solving abilities, decision-making skills, and adaptability.

- **Work Scenarios:** Here, candidates encounter hypothetical but realistic work-related situations. Their responses shed light on their judgment, prioritization skills, and capacity to handle the multi-faceted aspects of mail delivery.

The Significance of Preparation

Given the comprehensive nature of Exam 474, adequate preparation becomes non-negotiable. Not only does it help candidates familiarize themselves with the test format, but it also provides insights into the intricacies of a mail carrier's responsibilities. Reviewing guidelines provided by the U.S. Postal Service, participating in mock tests, and understanding the role's demands can significantly bolster a candidate's performance.

Deciphering the Scoring Mechanism

Scoring for Exam 474 is about more than just right or wrong answers. It delves deeper to understand a candidate's fit for the mail carrier role. Scores often reflect a candidate's relative performance compared to others, ensuring that only the most suitable individuals are cut.

A holistic review process ensures fairness and comprehensiveness, with high scores paving the way for the following stages of the selection process.

The Road Ahead: Post-Examination Steps

Upon completing Exam 474, candidates enter a pool of potential hires. However, the journey doesn't end there. Background checks, physical examinations, and further training sessions await those who clear the VEA.

The rigorous nature of the entire process underscores the U.S. Postal Service's commitment to maintaining its high standards and ensuring that every mail carrier dons not just a uniform but a mantle of responsibility, dedication, and public trust.

In a world dominated by digital communication, the tangible touch of a letter, the anticipation of a package, or the joy of a greeting card remains unparalleled. Behind every piece of mail lies the dedication and hard work of a mail carrier, a true unsung hero.

Exam 474, with its meticulous design and comprehensive evaluation criteria, ensures that this legacy of trust and efficiency remains unbroken. For every aspiring mail carrier, this exam isn't just a gateway to a job but an initiation into a tradition of excellence.

Mail Delivery Protocols: Proper Handling and Delivery Techniques

In the vast mosaic of the American landscape, mail carriers are vital threads weaving together communities, businesses, and individuals. From the snow-laden paths of the Northeast to the sun-drenched streets of the Southwest, they ensure that mail reaches its destination promptly and securely.

Yet, behind this seamless operation lies a sophisticated set of protocols and techniques that govern the process of mail handling and delivery. This section delves deep into these essential practices that uphold the trust and efficiency associated with the U.S. Postal Service.

The Imperative of Proper Mail Handling

Every day, the U.S. Postal Service processes millions of mail items. The vast array, from letters to parcels, demands intricate handling techniques to guarantee their integrity and safety. Proper mail handling starts long before a mail carrier exits the post office.

- **Sort and Sequence:** The initial phase involves sorting the mail according to the delivery route. Advanced automated machines assist in categorizing mail based on size, weight, and destination. Once sorted, the mail undergoes sequencing, aligning it in the exact delivery order. This meticulous organization ensures that mail carriers can efficiently deliver items without unnecessary delays or backtracking.

- **Safety First:** Mail carriers must remain vigilant about potential hazards. Sharp objects, leaking packages, or any suspicious items mandate immediate attention. Utilizing protective gloves, especially when handling parcels or bulkier things, reduces the risk of injuries.

- **Environmental Considerations:** Given the sensitive nature of certain mail items, such as medical prescriptions or perishable goods, carriers must consider environmental conditions. For instance, it's crucial to shield heat-sensitive items from direct sunlight in hot weather. Conversely, waterproof containers or protective coverings become indispensable during rain or snow to prevent water damage.

Efficient Delivery Techniques

Once prepared, the actual delivery requires a blend of skill, awareness, and precision. Here's how mail carriers ensure each item reaches its intended recipient securely:

- **Navigating the Route:** While familiarity offers an advantage, carriers leverage technology to streamline their journey. GPS devices, route optimization software, and digital maps assist in navigating complex areas, identifying shortcuts, and updating routes based on traffic conditions or road closures.

- **Delivering to Varied Mail Receptacles:** From standalone mailboxes to centralized mail units in apartment complexes, carriers encounter a range of receptacles. They must ensure that mail fits snugly, preventing theft or accidental loss. In situations where larger packages don't fit, carriers either place them in a secure location, such as a porch or a reception desk or leave a notice for the recipient, guiding them on how to retrieve their package.

- **Interacting with the Public:** Mail carriers often serve as the face of the U.S. Postal Service, interacting with customers daily. This interaction demands courtesy, patience, and clarity. Whether it's acquiring a signature for a registered mail or answering queries, carriers maintain professionalism, ensuring customer satisfaction.

- **Addressing Undeliverable Mail:** Occasionally, carriers encounter mail items marked for inaccessible or non-existent addresses. In such cases, they adhere to the protocol of returning the item to the post office and categorizing it as "undeliverable." Subsequent steps involve re-routing the mail or notifying the sender of the delivery challenge.

Ethical Standards and Confidentiality

The unwavering commitment to confidentiality and ethics lies at the heart of mail delivery. Carriers understand the sanctity of personal communication and take measures to uphold it:

- **Avoiding Tampering:** A carrier should not tamper with or open mail that doesn't belong to them. Even if a package seems damaged, the protocol dictates reporting it rather than attempting to inspect its contents.

- **Preserving Confidentiality:** On occasions where carriers interact with mail recipients, they must refrain from divulging details about other deliveries or discussing the nature of mail items.

Continuous Training and Upgradation

The world of mail delivery is dynamic. With evolving technologies, changing customer expectations, and new challenges, carriers often undergo continuous training. These sessions keep them abreast of the latest protocols, introduce them to emerging tools, and sharpen their problem-solving skills.

The role of a mail carrier extends beyond the mere delivery of items. It encompasses a deep understanding of procedures, a commitment to ethics, and a passion for serving the community. By adhering to the established mail handling and delivery protocols, carriers not only uphold the prestigious legacy of the U.S. Postal Service but also reinforce the trust millions place in them daily.

In the dance of communication, they play an indispensable role, ensuring every note, letter, or package finds its rhythm and reaches its intended stage.

Route Efficiency: Learning and Optimizing Delivery Routes

Within the scope of mail delivery, one of the most crucial aspects that often goes overlooked is the importance of route efficiency. A mail carrier entrusted with ensuring timely and accurate delivery has much to gain from understanding and optimizing its delivery routes. This streamlines the process and significantly enhances productivity, reduces costs, and boosts customer satisfaction.

The Anatomy of Route Efficiency

One must first discern its multi-faceted components to grasp the essence of route efficiency. An efficient route means the shortest and fastest path, but there's more to it than mere distance. It encompasses traffic patterns, geographical challenges, time constraints, and even interpersonal dynamics with recipients.

Why Prioritize Efficiency?

An efficient route directly correlates with several tangible and intangible benefits:

- **Time Conservation:** Time, the proverbial "money," is especially true for mail carriers. An optimized route invariably leads to quicker deliveries, allowing runners to handle more routes or take on additional tasks.

- **Fuel Economy:** As routes become streamlined, there's a direct reduction in the distance covered, leading to significant savings on fuel. This slashes operational costs and marks a step towards environmental sustainability.

- **Enhanced Customer Satisfaction:** Timely delivery fosters trust and satisfaction among recipients. Predictable and consistent mail delivery times can set a benchmark, leading to a heightened sense of reliability.

- **Reduction in Wear and Tear:** Lesser time on the road translates to reduced wear and tear on vehicles. This prolongs the vehicle's life, minimizes maintenance expenses, and ensures safety.

Strategies for Achieving Route Efficiency

Route efficiency only emerges after some time. It's an iterative process, continually evolving and adapting to changes. Here's how mail carriers can learn and hone their routes:

- **Leverage Technology:** Modern route planning software harnesses algorithms to compute the most efficient routes. Carriers can generate optimized paths by inputting data points like delivery addresses, time windows, and vehicle capacities. Additionally, real-time GPS tracking can alert carriers about sudden roadblocks or traffic surges, enabling on-the-spot route adjustments.

- **Understand the Terrain:** Every region, whether urban jungles or pastoral countryside, poses unique challenges. A deep understanding of local terrains, weather patterns, and road conditions can be invaluable. Over time, carriers intuitively discern shortcuts, avoid pothole-laden streets, or preempt traffic congestion based on specific times or events.

- **Build Rapport with Customers:** A good relationship with recipients can significantly smoothen deliveries. Regular customers can provide insights on when they're available, preferred delivery spots, or even tips on navigating their locality. This interpersonal dynamic, while seemingly minor, can compound over time, leading to notable efficiency gains.

- **Batch Deliveries:** Whenever possible, clustering deliveries can be a game-changer. If a carrier has multiple parcels for a single building or a closely-knit area, delivering them in a single trip rather than multiple rounds is prudent.

- **Continuous Feedback and Learning:** No system is perfect. Regular feedback, both from customers and self-evaluation, can illuminate areas of improvement. A newly opened road offers a quicker path, or a previously favored shortcut is now perennially congested. Being receptive to and proactively seeking such feedback can perpetually refine the efficiency of the route.

Challenges to Route Efficiency and Overcoming Them

While the quest for the perfect route is ongoing, carriers invariably encounter challenges:

- **Dynamic Variables:** Unexpected variables, like road construction, accidents, or public events, can disrupt even the most well-planned routes. The key lies in adaptability. Utilizing real-time traffic updates and local advisories can help navigate these disruptions.

- **Physical and Mental Fatigue:** The sheer repetitiveness and physical demands of the job can lead to fatigue. Regular breaks, ergonomic vehicle setups, and mental wellness practices can mitigate this. Furthermore, an efficient route inherently reduces the strain on the carrier.

- **Complex Deliveries:** Some deliveries, like large parcels or those requiring intricate setups, are inherently tricky. Preemptive communication with customers, understanding specific requirements, and occasionally seeking assistance can simplify these complexities.

Looking Ahead: The Future of Route Efficiency

With technological advancements, the horizon of route efficiency is rapidly expanding. Drone deliveries, electric vehicles with intelligent navigation systems, and advanced AI-driven route optimization algorithms are set to revolutionize the landscape.

For mail carriers, staying abreast of these developments while grounding themselves in the foundational principles of route efficiency will be instrumental.

Every step, turn, and pause counts in the intricate ballet of mail delivery. Route efficiency, therefore, stands as the choreography that orchestrates this dance to perfection.

As mail carriers crisscross the tapestry of American neighborhoods, their commitment to efficiency not only ensures that every letter, postcard, or package reaches its destination on time but also underscores the timeless ethos of the U.S. Postal Service: binding the nation together, one delivery at a time.

SAFETY: BEST PRACTICES FOR SAFE MAIL DELIVERY

In the hustle and rhythm of ensuring that mail and packages reach their intended recipients punctually, it's paramount for mail carriers to prioritize their safety and the safety of the communities they serve. Their role isn't just about connecting people through letters, parcels, and postcards; it's also about demonstrating a commitment to the well-being of all involved. Let's delve deeper into the best practices that champion safe mail delivery.

1. Personal Protective Equipment (PPE)

When we reflect on safety, our minds often journey to the realms of heavy industries and construction sites, but the mail delivery arena also necessitates using PPE.

- **Footwear:** Given the extensive walking and sometimes challenging terrains they navigate, mail carriers must choose footwear that offers both comfort and protection. Slip-resistant shoes can differ between a regular day and an unfortunate mishap, especially in rainy or snowy conditions.
- **Weather-appropriate attire:** Carriers face the wrath and benevolence of every season. Wearing UV-protected clothing during scorching summers, waterproof apparel during rains, and insulated garments during frigid winters can safeguard against environmental risks.

2. Ergonomic Practices

Regular lifting, bending, and walking become routine for a mail carrier. Over time, these actions can strain the body.

- **Lifting Techniques:** Understanding the science of body mechanics is crucial. When lifting heavier parcels, carriers should always bend their knees and use their legs, not their backs. Keeping packages close to the body while raising also minimizes strain.
- **Bag Positioning:** For those who use shoulder bags, alternating the bag's position between shoulders at regular intervals can prevent muscle imbalances.

3. Vehicular Safety

For those routes that require vehicles:

- **Regular Maintenance:** Like any machine, maintenance is critical. Regular checks on brakes, tires, and lights ensure the vehicle remains in optimal condition.
- **Defensive Driving:** Given that mail carriers often operate in residential areas with children playing and pets around, adopting a defensive driving approach is prudent. This means anticipating potential hazards and always being prepared to react.

4. Canine Caution

Dogs, often protective of their territories, can pose challenges.

- **Reading Canine Body Language:** Recognizing signs of aggression or fear in dogs can be lifesaving. A wagging tail might seem friendly, but combined with other signals, it might indicate agitation.
- **Use of Deterrents:** While harming an animal is a last resort, carriers should be equipped with safe canine deterrent sprays for emergencies.

5. Weather Woes

Weather conditions can be unpredictable and can change the dynamics of mail delivery.

- **Slip and Fall Prevention:** Wet leaves, icy patches, or even unexpected puddles can be slip hazards. Being vigilant and treading cautiously can avert potential falls.
- **Staying Hydrated:** Carriers should consume ample water on sweltering days to fend off dehydration.

6. Situational Awareness

Being aware of surroundings is about more than efficient delivery and safety.

- **Know the Route:** Familiarity with the route allows carriers to anticipate challenges, be it a broken sidewalk or a house with an overly protective dog.
- **Stay Alert:** Keeping an ear out for unusual sounds or disturbances and an eye out for any unusual activity can ensure personal safety.

7. Handling Hazardous Packages

On the rare occasion that a carrier might come across a package that seems suspicious:

- **Do Not Open:** If a package is leaking, has a peculiar odor, or displays any other signs of being hazardous, it's best not to open it.
- **Immediate Reporting:** Such parcels should be reported immediately to superiors, ensuring they are isolated from other deliveries.

8. Communication Channels

A robust communication channel between mail carriers and their central offices can be a linchpin in ensuring safety.

- **Regular Check-ins:** P periodic check-ins can act as a safety net, especially in adverse weather conditions or during late hours.
- **Emergency Protocols:** It is crucial to know who to call and what steps to take in case of emergencies – be it medical, vehicular, or any other –.

9. Respect Private Property

Mail carriers are granted unique access to private properties.

- **Gate Etiquette:** Always ensure gates are closed behind, especially in properties with pets.
- **Avoiding Sensitive Areas:** Staying clear of areas like swimming pools, trampolines, or any other potential hazard areas on a property ensures the safety of both the carrier and the residents.

10. Mental Health Matters

The job's repetitive nature, physical demands, and environmental challenges can take a toll on mental health.

- **Regular Breaks:** Taking short breaks to rest and rejuvenate can aid in maintaining mental alertness.
- **Seek Support:** If feeling overwhelmed, carriers should not hesitate to seek professional counseling or talk to a colleague or supervisor.

The tapestry of mail delivery, woven with commitment, diligence, and community service threads, is as much about connecting people as it is about safeguarding the connectors – the mail carriers. By adhering to the best safety practices, carriers protect themselves and uphold the integrity and trust associated with their profession.

EXAM 475 - MAIL HANDLER VEA

The Postal Service, with its vast network and dynamic operations, remains a crucial linchpin in the intricate web of American communication. With each passing year, the demand for efficient, effective, and dedicated individuals to join this mammoth organization rises, and so does the need for tests that screen the potential candidates for these roles. Among the variety of exams the Postal Service employs to assess its prospective employees, Exam 475 - Mail Handler VEA stands out prominently. Designed meticulously to gauge the capabilities of those aspiring to be mail handlers, this examination reflects the core tenets and responsibilities associated with the position.

Nature of the Mail Handler Role

Before plunging into the specifics of Exam 475, understanding the role of a mail handler is paramount. Mail handlers, as the name evocatively suggests, are involved in the manual handling of mail. This task, seemingly straightforward, encapsulates a myriad of responsibilities. From loading and unloading mail to and from vehicles to moving and organizing mail within processing centers, mail handlers stand at the intersection of speed, accuracy, and dexterity.

Core Components of Exam 475

While the exam, at its essence, evaluates the fundamental competencies required of a mail handler, it does so through a combination of diverse sections, each crafted to assess a specific skill set.

1. Reading and Comprehension

Many of the mail handler's job involves reading labels, addresses, and instructions. Therefore, this section delves into the candidate's ability to swiftly comprehend and interpret written instructions. It will often present scenarios or passages that emulate the situations a mail handler might face and then pose questions to test comprehension.

2. Memory and Number Sequencing

Given the vast mail volumes, mail handlers must demonstrate a keen sense of order and sequence. This section assesses the candidate's ability to remember specific details from provided information and to recognize and establish numerical lines, a skill vital when sorting mail according to postal codes or other criteria.

3. Safety Procedures and Protocols

No postal facility downplays the importance of safety. This section is dedicated to evaluating a candidate's awareness and understanding of basic safety protocols, especially those pertinent to the handling and processing mail. It might include questions about how to lift heavy objects, handle machinery, or respond to potential hazards in the workspace.

4. Spatial Orientation

Often, mail handlers need to gauge the size of a package, determine how it might fit in a specific space, or figure out the best way to organize a set of boxes in a limited area. This section tests spatial intelligence and the ability to manipulate objects mentally, determining how they fit together.

5. Personal Assessment and Experience Inventory

Unlike the other sections, this is more introspective and seeks to understand the candidate's previous experiences, disposition, and approach to challenges. Questions range from how one handled a challenging job situation before gauging one's teamwork and collaboration skills.

The Impetus behind Exam 475

Why does the Postal Service emphasize an exam for a mail handler's position? The answer lies in the intricate and high-stakes nature of the job. Despite the advent of electronic communication, a significant chunk of America still relies on traditional mail for many needs. The primary spectrum varies from legal documents to personal letters, business packages, and sentimental gifts. A single mistake could mean a critical medication doesn't reach a patient on time or a legal document gets lost, leading to significant repercussions. Therefore, the Postal Service ensures through Exam 475 that every mail handler it employs is proficient and embodies the ethos of responsibility and dedication the job demands.

Preparation and Approach

Given the comprehensive nature of Exam 475, preparation becomes pivotal. Candidates are advised to familiarize themselves with the basics of postal operations, particularly those related to mail handling. Reading manuals, watching documentaries, or speaking to current or former mail handlers can provide invaluable insights. Mock tests in various formats can help gauge one's current proficiency and highlight areas requiring additional focus.

However, beyond the exam specifics, an aspirant must understand and embrace the spirit of the role. Being a mail handler isn't just about physical stamina or quick reading; it's about being a cog in the vast machinery that connects people, businesses, and institutions. It's about understanding the silent stories each package or letter carries and ensuring they reach their destination seamlessly.

Exam 475 - Mail Handler VEA isn't just a test; it's a testament to the Postal Service's commitment to upholding the highest standards in its operations. Everyone who clears this exam and dons the role of a mail handler doesn't just take on a job; they take on the mantle of trust, reliability, and connection.

Mail Sorting: Techniques and Equipment for Efficient Mail Sorting

The world of mail is vast and intricate. Each day, countless letters, parcels, and packages crisscross cities, states, and countries, each bearing its own story, purpose, and destination. At the heart of ensuring that each piece reaches its intended recipient lies the art and science of mail sorting. Intricate as a dance precise as a surgical procedure, mail sorting is both an art form and a logistical marvel.

Understanding Mail Sorting

Mail sorting is not merely about placing letters in different bins. It's a process that ensures a letter dropped into a mailbox in one part of the country reaches a small apartment or a business on the other side, sometimes even across oceans. This journey is streamlined and made efficient through advanced techniques and cutting-edge equipment.

Techniques for Efficient Mail Sorting

1. Manual Sorting

In the age before technological advances in the postal sector, mail sorting was predominantly manual. Skilled workers with a deep knowledge of geographic areas would sort mail by hand. They'd categorize letters based on cities, then further break them down into neighborhoods, streets, and individual addresses. While manual sorting still plays a role in certain niche areas or smaller postal offices, automated methods are increasingly being complemented or replaced.

2. Barcode Recognition

Each piece of mail today gets stamped with a barcode that encapsulates a plethora of information, including its destination. Advanced scanners read these barcodes, quickly determining where each letter or package should go. This method drastically reduces sorting time and enhances accuracy.

3. Optical Character Recognition (OCR)

Modern sorting facilities employ OCR technologies capable of reading handwritten or printed addresses. These machines scan the face of each mail piece, interpret the address, and then rapidly direct the mail to its intended destination, be it a nearby town or a distant state.

4. Shape Sorting

Not all mail is uniform. There are letters, postcards, boxes, and even tubes. Advanced sorting systems can identify the shape and size of mail pieces, sorting them accordingly. This technique ensures that letters are outside of parcel bins and vice versa.

Equipment that Powers Mail Sorting

The leap from manual sorting to today's high-speed, highly accurate methods has been driven by sophisticated equipment. Some of the game-changers in this arena include:

1. Flat Sorting Machines

These are designed primarily for letters and flat envelopes. They operate at impressive speeds, often sorting thousands of letters in an hour. Equipped with OCR and barcode reading capabilities, they rapidly categorize mail based on destination.

2. Parcel Sorting Systems

Due to their varied sizes and shapes, packages require a different sorting approach. Modern parcel sorters can handle many packages, from tiny boxes to larger parcels. These systems use conveyor belts, scanners, and advanced software to ensure each packet is routed correctly.

3. Tilt-Tray Sorters

Imagine a system where mail pieces are placed on trays. As these trays move along a conveyor, they approach the designated drop point for each article. Once there, the tray tilts, gently dropping the mail into the correct bin. This is the magic of tilt-tray sorters, known for their efficiency and gentleness.

4. Automated Mail Bundlers

Post sorting, before the mail heads out for delivery, it needs bundling. Automated bundlers collate sorted mail, grouping them for easier delivery. This streamlines the process for mail carriers, ensuring they spend minimal time at the postal facility and more on their routes.

The Human Touch in a Machine-driven Process

While machines and technologies have redefined the mail-sorting landscape, human oversight remains invaluable. With their keen eyes and years of experience, postal workers oversee these automated processes. They step in when machines falter, when a barcode is smudged, or when an address is too faded. They ensure that while engines drive efficiency, the human touch ensures reliability.

The Future of Mail Sorting

As with many sectors, the postal world continues to evolve. With the rise of e-commerce, the volume of parcels is on an upward trajectory. This demands even more efficient sorting systems. Innovations in artificial intelligence, machine learning, and robotics herald the next wave of sorting equipment. These systems will not only sort mail but also predict flow patterns, optimize routes, and even interface directly with senders and recipients, enhancing transparency.

Mail sorting, at its core, embodies the essence of communication. It bridges a sender's intent and a recipient's anticipation. The postal service ensures this bridge is robust, reliable, and efficient through a blend of techniques and state-of-the-art equipment. As we send off a letter or receive a package, we rarely pause to think of the marvels of sorting that operate behind the scenes. Yet, this intricate ballet, performed tirelessly day in and day out, keeps our world connected, one piece of mail at a time.

Safety Procedures: Best Practices in a Mail Facility Environment

Working within a mail facility requires more than understanding the intricate web of mail routing, sorting, and delivery. It mandates a rigorous adherence to safety protocols to ensure employees' well-being and the mail's integrity. A mail facility is a dynamic space bustling with movement, machinery, and human interaction. Navigating such a setting safely is paramount to the success of the postal operation.

Understanding the Risks

Before delving into the best practices, we must understand the risks associated with a mail facility environment. Heavy machinery operates in close quarters, employees are constantly on the move, and the volume of mail can be overwhelming. This milieu can be a potential source of injuries or mishaps if not handled with care. Moreover, specific parcels might contain hazardous materials, requiring special handling.

Ground Rules for Safety

1. Training is Non-Negotiable

Every employee, regardless of their role, must undergo comprehensive safety training. This isn't a one-off endeavor. Regular refresher courses and updates on new safety protocols are essential. Training imparts knowledge of equipment operation, emergency protocols, and hazard recognition, ensuring employees remain vigilant.

2. Prioritizing Ergonomics

Repetitive tasks, like lifting parcels or standing for extended periods, can take a toll on the body. Emphasizing ergonomics means designing workspaces and functions that cater to human capabilities and limitations. Ergonomic chairs, adjustable workstations, and proper lifting techniques can mitigate the risk of musculoskeletal injuries.

3. Machinery Safety

The mechanized aspect of mail sorting cannot be stressed enough. With machines playing a pivotal role, understanding their safe operation is critical. Regular maintenance checks, ensuring machinery guards are in place, and immediate reporting of any malfunctions are steps that reduce the risk of accidents.

4. Hazardous Material Handling

Not every piece of mail is benign. Some parcels may contain substances that are flammable, toxic, or corrosive. Employees need to be adept at recognizing such boxes, either by their labeling or the information provided by the sender. Such mail must be isolated and handled with appropriate protective gear, ensuring no harm to the staff or the facility.

5. Footwear and Clothing

The proper attire can make a difference. Non-slip shoes can prevent falls, especially when the floor is slick from spills. Loose clothing should be avoided as it can get caught in machinery. Some facilities also mandate using safety vests to enhance visibility, especially in areas with vehicular movement.

6. Fire Safety Protocols

Given the volume of paper and parcels, mail facilities can be vulnerable to fires. Regular checks of fire safety equipment, clear evacuation routes, and training on fire safety can be the difference between a minor incident and a major catastrophe.

7. Maintaining Hygiene and Cleanliness

A cluttered workspace is a hazard. It's not just about tripping over a stray parcel but also about ensuring no dust or debris buildup might impact machinery or become a fire risk. Regular cleaning, waste disposal, and ensuring walkways remain clear are simple yet effective measures.

Safety in the Age of Technology

The advent of technology has added another layer to safety protocols. Automated machinery comes with its own set of safety guidelines. Ensuring employees understand these and are trained to handle emergencies is crucial. Moreover, in an era where cybersecurity threats loom, mail facilities must secure their digital infrastructure. A breach could compromise operational data and sensitive information about recipients and senders.

Creating a Culture of Safety

While protocols and guidelines form the bedrock of safety, the real difference is made by creating a culture that prioritizes well-being. A culture where employees look out for each other, near-misses are reported and analyzed, and safety is seen not as a mandate but as an integral part of the job.

Continuous Evaluation and Feedback

Safety isn't static. As operations evolve, so do potential risks. Regular safety audits and employee feedback can help identify potential areas of concern. This proactive approach, rather than reactive, ensures that potential hazards are nipped in the bud.

The intricate dance of mail sorting, routing, and delivery is awe-inspiring. But ensuring this dance is performed safely is equally, if not more, crucial. A mail facility that prioritizes the safety of its employees, the integrity of its operations, and the well-being of its mail stand as a beacon of operational excellence. Safety in such an environment is not just a guideline—it's a way of life.

Equipment Maintenance: Basic Upkeep of Mail Handling Machinery

At the heart of every efficient mail facility lies a cadre of machinery that hums in perfect symphony, ensuring that each piece of mail finds its rightful place. However, like every orchestra requires tuning, mail-handling machinery demands regular maintenance to function at its peak. The role of equipment maintenance in the postal sector must be considered. It ensures not just operational efficiency but also the safety of the workforce and the integrity of the mail being processed.

Understanding the Machinery Landscape

Mail handling machinery is a broad term that encompasses a range of equipment. The spectrum is vast, from conveyor systems that move mail seamlessly across the facility to advanced sorting machines that use optical character recognition to categorize mail. There are also label applicators, stamp-canceling devices, and bundling systems that wrap packages. Each of these machines has its own set of maintenance requirements.

The Imperative of Regular Maintenance

Every piece of machinery, over time, undergoes wear and tear. Regular maintenance is a countermeasure, ensuring minor issues don't escalate into major malfunctions. There are several reasons why equipment maintenance is non-negotiable:

1. Prolonged Equipment Lifespan

Machines are a significant investment. Regular upkeep ensures they function optimally and extend their operational life. This means reduced overheads in the long run as the frequency of machinery replacement decreases.

2. Operational Efficiency

Well-maintained machinery operates at its peak. This translates to faster mail processing, reduced bottlenecks, and a smoother workflow. In a domain where time is of the essence, equipment efficiency can be the difference between on-time delivery and delays.

3. Safety Assurance

Malfunctioning equipment isn't just an operational hazard; it's a safety risk. The implications can be severe, whether it's a conveyor belt that's misaligned or a sorting machine that jams frequently. Regular maintenance checks and prompt repairs reduce the risk of accidents, safeguarding employees.

Critical Elements of Equipment Maintenance

Maintenance isn't just about fixing something when it breaks. It's a holistic approach that involves several stages:

1. Preventive Maintenance

This proactive approach involves routinely checking machines for signs of wear, even if they appear to function normally. Think of it as a medical check-up for machinery. It includes tasks like lubricating moving parts, replacing worn-out belts, or recalibrating sensors. The goal is to catch potential issues before they escalate.

2. Corrective Maintenance

Unlike preventive maintenance, corrective maintenance addresses evident machinery malfunctions. It's a reactive approach that comes into play when a machine breaks down or doesn't function as expected.

3. Predictive Maintenance

With technological advancements, especially in the Internet of Things (IoT), machines can self-monitor. Sensors embedded within can predict when a component might fail or when maintenance is due. This data-driven approach can significantly optimize the maintenance process.

4. Maintenance Documentation

Every maintenance task, whether preventive or corrective, needs documentation. Maintaining a record helps track machinery health, identify recurrent issues, and plan future maintenance schedules.

Human Element in Equipment Maintenance

While machines form the core of mail processing, the human element cannot be sidelined. With their keen eye and experience, skilled technicians play a pivotal role in equipment maintenance. Their expertise can often spot issues that sensors might miss. Regular training sessions, workshops, and certification courses can ensure these technicians stay updated with the latest machinery advancements.

Embracing Technology in Maintenance

Beyond the predictive maintenance offered by IoT, technology plays a broader role in machinery upkeep. Advanced diagnostics tools can provide a deep dive into machinery health; software updates can enhance machine functionality, and digital maintenance logs can streamline documentation.

Challenges in Equipment Maintenance

Despite its evident importance, maintenance does come with its set of challenges. Scheduling maintenance without disrupting operations, sourcing genuine replacement parts, or staying updated with rapidly evolving machinery tech can be daunting. However, these challenges can be effectively addressed with a robust maintenance strategy.

In the grand tapestry of mail processing, machinery stands out as the linchpin and the workhorse. Ensuring its upkeep is not just a task but an imperative. With its blend of human expertise and technological aid, equipment maintenance ensures that the postal orchestra plays uninterrupted and in perfect harmony.

Package Handling: Special Considerations for Parcels and Large Items

In the fast-paced world of mail handling, emphasizing the swift and accurate processing of letters often steals the spotlight. However, nestled within the bustling environment of a mail facility lies an equally essential task, though it demands a different set of considerations: package handling. Parcels and more oversized items present unique challenges, requiring physical dexterity and a nuanced understanding of the factors that govern their safe and effective processing.

The Rise of the Package Era

With the digital revolution reshaping the shopping habits of millions, e-commerce has brought about an explosion in the volume of packages being dispatched worldwide. This surge underscores the need for robust strategies and guidelines for parcel handling. After all, each box tells a story, often of personal significance to its recipient, whether it's a birthday gift, medical supplies, or essential documents.

Physical Challenges in Handling Large Items

By their very nature, parcels come in diverse shapes, sizes, and weights. Unlike standardized letters, each package demands a tailored approach:

1. Weight Considerations

Heavier parcels require techniques that reduce strain on the handler. Lifting with the knees, keeping the package close to the body, and using both hands are fundamentals that every handler should internalize. It's not just about ensuring the package's safety but also about safeguarding the employee's well-being.

2. Size and Shape Variances

Large or irregularly shaped items can be cumbersome. Equipment such as trolleys or hand trucks can aid their transportation. Additionally, understanding the package's fragile or liquid contents can influence how the handler approaches its movement.

Technological Innovations in Package Handling

Modern mail facilities increasingly turn to technology to streamline the handling of more oversized items:

1. Conveyor Systems

Advanced conveyor systems, equipped with sensors, can sort packages based on size and destination. These systems reduce manual handling, thus minimizing the potential for damage or misplacement.

2. Robotics and Automation

Robotic arms and automated guided vehicles (AGVs) are making inroads into the mail industry. They can lift and transport heavy or oversized parcels precisely, ensuring efficiency and safety.

The Delicate Dance of Fragile Items

Not all packages are made equal. Fragile items, whether they are delicate electronics, glassware, or medical equipment, require an added layer of care:

1. Signage and Labels

Marked labels indicating the fragile nature of the package are essential. These act as visual cues for handlers, prompting them to exercise caution.

2. Specialized Packing Materials

Bubble wrap, foam inserts, and reinforced boxes are crucial in protecting the contents of fragile parcels. Handlers should be trained to recognize and respect these packing choices.

3. Designated Fragile Zones

Some facilities designate particular areas for the processing of fragile packages. These zones, free of potential hazards, ensure that delicate items remain undamaged during their journey.

Security Measures in Package Handling

The world of parcels isn't just about physical considerations; it also dives deep into security. With the rise in the shipment of high-value items, security measures have become paramount:

1. Package Scanning

Advanced scanning equipment can detect potentially hazardous or prohibited items within parcels. This ensures the facility's safety and aids in thwarting illicit activities.

2. Track and Trace Systems

Modern packages often come embedded with tracking chips or barcodes. These allow both the sender and recipient to monitor the package's journey, ensuring transparency and reducing the likelihood of theft or misplacement.

3. Sealed Transport Units

For high-value or sensitive shipments, sealed transport units or containers provide an added layer of security. These seals are tamper-evident, signaling any unauthorized access.

Environmental Considerations

As awareness about environmental sustainability grows, package handling also delves into eco-friendly practices:

1. Reusable Packaging

More shippers are adopting reusable packaging materials, be it sturdy boxes or fabric pouches. Handlers should be trained to recognize and return these materials for reuse.

2. Eco-friendly Packing Materials

From biodegradable peanuts to recycled paper padding, green packing choices are rising. Understanding their significance and ensuring they remain intact is crucial.

Handling parcels, significantly larger or unique items isn't just a task; it's an art form. It demands a blend of physical skill, technological aid, and a profound understanding of each package's nuances. As the world leans more into the digital realm and e-commerce continues its upward trajectory, the mastery of package handling remains a cornerstone in the tapestry of modern mail operations.

EXAM 477 - CUSTOMER SERVICE/CLERK VEA

Diving into the world of mail services, it becomes apparent that there's another essential dimension: the human connection behind the vast infrastructure of mail transport and package handling. At the core of this intricate web stands the formidable pillar of customer service, and playing a crucial role within this realm is the position defined by the Customer Service/Clerk Virtual Entry Assessment or Exam 477. This comprehensive guide aims to delve into the nuances of this exam, painting a vivid picture of its significance, structure, and strategies for success.

Exam 477, while intricately technical in its approach, fundamentally tests a candidate's aptitude for building and maintaining human relationships in a professional setting. Its primary objective is to identify individuals with the necessary skills and temperament to serve as practical clerks and customer service representatives within the postal service framework.

Why Customer Service Matters

Mail and package delivery is more than just a logistical endeavor; it's a service that connects people, delivers emotions, and sometimes meets critical needs. Customer service representatives and clerks serve as the face of this vast enterprise, ensuring that every interaction is smooth, satisfactory, and solution-oriented.

The Structure of Exam 477

Understanding the exam's architecture gives aspirants a road map for their preparation journey. Exam 477, while rooted in customer service, also extends its tendrils into operational understanding and situational judgment.

Personal Characteristics and Experience Inventory

In this segment, candidates encounter questions probing their personal and professional experiences, gauging their reactions and approaches to diverse scenarios typical of a customer service setting. This section isn't just about right or wrong answers; it's about consistency, integrity, and a genuine affinity for customer-centric solutions.

Virtual Entry Assessment - MC (477)

Here, candidates grapple with multiple-choice questions, each sculpted to evaluate their problem-solving abilities, attention to detail, and understanding of customer service dynamics. It's a whirlwind tour through simulated challenges, demanding quick thinking and effective decision-making.

Mastering the Exam: Essential Strategies

Tackling Exam 477 requires a blend of preparation, presence of mind, and a deep-seated understanding of customer service tenets.

Empathy: The Golden Thread

In the universe of customer service, empathy reigns supreme. Whether addressing a concern, resolving a dispute, or simply guiding a customer, the ability to put oneself in another's shoes can be a game-changer. As candidates navigate the intricacies of Exam 477, keeping empathy as the guiding star can pave the way for authentic and effective responses.

Operational Acumen

While interpersonal skills are undeniably crucial, they must be complemented with a solid understanding of operational protocols and processes. A representative who can seamlessly merge their people skills with process knowledge is a force to be reckoned with.

Situational Judgement

Life is an ever-evolving tapestry of situations, especially in a customer-facing role. Some are routine, while others are unprecedented. Exam 477 significantly emphasizes gauging a candidate's judgment in diverse scenarios. It's not about memorizing responses but developing an intuitive understanding of situations and reacting appropriately.

Post-Exam Dynamics: The Road Ahead

Passing Exam 477 is an accomplishment but merely the beginning of a vibrant journey. Those who emerge victorious from this assessment are poised to dive into a world where every day brings new challenges, fresh faces, and countless opportunities to make a difference.

Training and Skill Enhancement

Clearing the exam paves the way for rigorous training sessions, where candidates polish their skills, understand the nitty-gritty of the postal system, and learn the art and science of delivering impeccable customer service.

The Dance of Daily Duties

Every day is a dance of diverse duties, from handling customer queries and managing operational challenges to coordinating with different departments and ensuring smooth service delivery. It's a dynamic role that demands flexibility, resilience and an unwavering commitment to customer satisfaction.

Exam 477, the Customer Service/Clerk VEA, is more than just an assessment; it's a gateway to a world where human connection meets operational excellence. In an age dominated by digital interactions, the human touch, epitomized by stellar customer service, becomes even more invaluable. For those aspiring to make a mark in this realm, mastering Exam 477 isn't just about securing a job; it's about embarking on a journey filled with challenges, learning, and countless moments of genuine human connection.

Retail Operations: Delving into USPS Products, Services, and Payment Methods

In postal services, retail operations connect the vast logistical infrastructure with the end consumers. In a realm where commerce meets customer service, retail operations within the USPS aren't just about sales but also about ensuring that every customer leaves with a positive experience. This section explored the products, services, and payment methods that define USPS's retail operations.

The Products: More Than Just Stamps

USPS's product portfolio offers various options tailored to meet diverse needs. Beyond the traditional stamp, a universe of products caters to varying mailing and shipping requirements.

Priority Mail

Crafted for those in a hurry, Priority Mail promises expedited delivery. It isn't just about speed, though. This service is about reliability, ensuring timely deliveries without compromising the package's or contents' integrity.

Media Mail

In an era defined by digital exchanges, the charm of tangible media - books, sound recordings, or educational material - remains unparalleled. Recognizing this, USPS's Media Mail service offers a cost-effective solution for shipping media products.

Flat Rate Boxes and Envelopes

Clarity in costs often translates to peace of mind. With USPS's flat rate offerings, customers have the assurance of a fixed price, irrespective of the package's weight. This simplicity, coupled with the availability of various box and envelope sizes, ensures flexibility and affordability.

The Services: Catering to Every Need

While products form the tangible backbone, the services offered by USPS breathe life into the retail experience, ensuring every customer finds a solution tailored to their unique needs.

Money Orders

In a world teeming with electronic transactions, the reliability and security of money orders continue to hold ground. As a safe alternative to checks and cash, USPS money orders provide a trusted method for payments and remittances.

Postal Savings and Financial Services

Understanding the financial pulse of the community, USPS extends services beyond mailing. From savings schemes to financial products tailored for specific demographics, these offerings blend the trustworthiness of the postal system with the nuances of finance.

Package Pickup and Redelivery

In the hustle and bustle of modern life, missed deliveries can be inconvenient. USPS's package pickup and redelivery services address this, ensuring that customers can receive their parcels at a time that suits them.

Payment Methods: Seamless and Diverse

The transaction's conclusion often rests on the payment in the retail environment. Recognizing the diversity in customer preferences, USPS has integrated many payment methods into its operations.

Cash and Check Transactions

Traditional yet timeless, cash and check transactions continue to be the bedrock of retail payments. With trained personnel adept at handling and verifying these transactions, customers can quickly complete their prices.

Card Payments

In the age of plastic money, card payments - credit or debit - have become the go-to choice for many. USPS's retail counters have state-of-the-art card processing units, ensuring secure and swift transactions.

Mobile and Digital Payments

Keeping pace with technological advancements, USPS has embraced digital payments. From mobile wallets to contactless transactions, these methods offer customers the convenience of swift payments without needing physical currency.

The Human Element: Building Trust and Relationships

Amid the myriad of products, services, and payment methods, the essence of USPS's retail operations rests on the human connection. Every transaction is an opportunity to build trust, to understand a need, and to offer a solution. It's not just about a sale; it's about ensuring that the customer feels seen, heard, and valued, whether they're sending a heartfelt letter or making a crucial payment.

USPS's retail operations are a testament to its commitment to serving its community. Every product, service, and payment method has a story - a story of understanding needs, offering solutions, and building lasting relationships. As the world evolves, with technologies transforming every facet of our lives, the essence of USPS's retail operations remains unshaken: an unwavering focus on the customer, blending the age-old values of trust and reliability with the dynamism of modern commerce.

CUSTOMER INTERACTIONS: EFFECTIVE COMMUNICATION AND PROBLEM RESOLUTION

Effective communication and problem-solving capabilities are the heart of every successful business interaction, especially within service-driven sectors like the USPS. Serving millions daily, the USPS encounters a myriad of inquiries, concerns, and feedback. But it's not merely the volume of interactions that matters—it's the depth and quality of each engagement. As customers walk into a post office or seek assistance, they're looking not only for solutions but also for empathy, understanding, and validation.

Before diving into problem-solving, one must master the art of listening. Active listening isn't just about hearing words; it's about grasping the nuances, understanding underlying emotions, and demonstrating genuine interest. It's an art that goes beyond nodding and making generic acknowledgments.

When a customer expresses frustration over a lost package or confusion regarding a service, it's imperative to acknowledge their feelings. Say, "I understand why you'd feel that way," rather than, "I understand." The difference might seem trivial, but the former recognizes the emotion and merely acknowledges a fact.

Clarity in Communication

Clear communication is pivotal. This involves explaining complex procedures in a manner that customers can comprehend. It's essential to avoid jargon or overly technical terms. For instance, instead of saying, "Your package underwent a transshipment," opt for, "Your package was moved through different transport modes or locations to reach its final destination." The goal is to simplify without diluting the accuracy of the information.

Empathy: The Bridge to Trust

Empathy involves putting oneself in the customer's shoes, feeling their concerns, and understanding their perspective. While it might not expedite a package's delivery, compassion can ease a customer's anxieties. Responding, "I can imagine how important this package is for you, and I'm here to help," fosters a connection that transcends transactional dynamics.

Offering Solutions, Not Excuses

In problem resolution, it's essential to pivot focus from what went wrong to how it can be rectified. Customers appreciate proactive solutions rather than prolonged explanations of the issue's genesis. If a package is delayed, instead of detailing logistical challenges, it's more beneficial to provide a revised delivery estimate and assure the customer of expedited processing.

Handling Difficult Conversations

Not all interactions are straightforward. Due to prior unsatisfactory experiences or heightened emotions, some customers can be particularly challenging. In such cases, patience becomes paramount. Avoid interrupting or becoming defensive. Instead, validate their feelings, apologize for inconveniences, and commit to a resolution.

Feedback: The Goldmine for Improvement

While positive feedback boosts morale, constructive criticism provides growth opportunities. Adopting a receptive stance towards suggestions or grievances can illuminate areas that might have been overlooked. For instance, if customers frequently express confusion over a specific form or procedure, it could signal the need for more precise guidelines or additional staff training.

Follow-up: Demonstrating Continued Care

Once a problem is resolved, the interaction shouldn't necessarily end. Following up with a customer to ensure they received their package or were satisfied with the solution provided underscores the commitment to exemplary service. It's a small gesture, but it leaves a lasting impression.

Harnessing Technology for Enhanced Interactions

Modern times have ushered in many technological tools that can amplify the quality of customer interactions. Chatbots can answer common queries instantly, while CRM (Customer Relationship Management) systems can store essential customer data, ensuring that every interaction is personalized and informed. Leveraging such tools while retaining the human touch can harmonize efficiency with empathy.

When navigated adeptly, customer interactions can transform challenges into opportunities and customers into advocates. Every question posed, every concern raised, and every feedback given paints a portrait of customer expectations. By listening actively, communicating with clarity, responding with empathy, and striving for genuine problem resolution, USPS can fortify its reputation as an institution that delivers mail and unparalleled customer experiences.

Inventory & Stock: Managing Retail and Postal Stock Items

Inventory and stock management remain crucial in any service-driven environment, particularly in sectors as demanding and high-volume as the postal service. Efficient handling of retail and postal stock items is not just about numbers—it's an intricate balance of timing, prediction, demand, and delivery. It dictates the tempo of operations and directly affects service quality. Here's a deep dive into the mechanisms and intricacies of inventory and stock management within a postal context.

Understanding the Significance

Why is inventory management pivotal for a postal entity? It's the backbone that supports two primary objectives: ensuring that necessary items are available when customers need them and minimizing the costs associated with stocking and storing. Be it stamps, envelopes, or packaging materials, adequate stock ensures that the service remains uninterrupted and customers leave satisfied.

Demand Forecasting: Predicting the Pulse

One of the first steps in stellar inventory management is accurately predicting demand. By analyzing historical data, current market trends, and seasonality, postal services can anticipate the volume of items they'll need. This ensures availability and prevents overstocking, which can tie up capital and waste resources. Imagine the increase in demand for seasonal things like holiday-themed stamps; predicting this surge ensures availability without leading to a surplus post-season.

The Just-In-Time Approach

The Just-In-Time (JIT) approach has garnered accolades for its efficiency in inventory management. By receiving goods only when they are needed, postal services can reduce inventory costs and minimize storage needs. However, this method requires precise coordination, timely deliveries, and an impeccable understanding of demand patterns.

Regular Audits: The Reality Check

Regularly auditing the stock is akin to a health check-up for inventory management. Discrepancies can be identified and rectified by assessing what's on the shelves versus what the records indicate. This not only ensures accuracy but also aids in identifying patterns—like recurrent shortages of a particular item, signaling a potential underestimation of its demand.

Safety Stock: The Buffer Against Uncertainties

Even with impeccable demand forecasting, the world of inventory is full of surprises. Hence, maintaining a safety stock is prudent. This is a buffer stock, ensuring that operations remain unaffected even if demand suddenly spikes or there's a delay in replenishment. However, deciding the volume of safety stock requires a delicate balance to avoid unnecessary accumulation.

Vendor Relationships: The Lifeline

Strong vendor relationships form the cornerstone of effective inventory management. Regular communication, transparent dealings, and timely payments ensure that when the postal service needs rapid restocking, vendors are willing and able to prioritize their requests. Moreover, long-term relationships can lead to favorable terms and discounts, further optimizing costs.

Embracing Technology

In the modern age, relying solely on manual methods for inventory management is not only cumbersome but also error-prone. Leveraging technology, from barcode scanning to sophisticated Inventory Management Systems (IMS), can streamline processes. Such systems can provide real-time data, automate reordering processes, and offer insights into demand patterns.

Waste Reduction and Sustainability

Effective inventory management also aligns with sustainability goals. By avoiding overstocking, the wastage of perishable items, like certain packaging materials, can be minimized. Furthermore, understanding stock movement can aid in optimizing transportation, leading to reduced carbon footprints.

Training and Skill Development

Lastly, it's vital to remember that systems and processes, no matter how advanced, are operated by humans. Regular training sessions ensure that the staff remains updated about best practices, understands the importance of their role in inventory management, and is adept at using technological tools.

Inventory and stock management, especially in the dynamic environment of postal services, is a dance of precision, anticipation, and adaptation. It's about understanding the rhythm of demand, having the agility to respond, and the foresight to prepare. As postal services evolve, with e-commerce integrations and global operations, inventory management will not just remain significant—it will become even more intricate and essential. The goal will always be twofold: ensuring customer satisfaction and optimizing operational efficiency. And with the right strategies, both are achievable in harmony.

Clerk Operations: Understanding Back-end Postal Operations and Tasks

Diving into the world of postal services reveals a complex, intricately woven tapestry of operations, with every thread playing its part in crafting the bigger picture. The postal clerk is one of the most pivotal roles in this vast network. Far removed from the often romanticized notion of stamp collections and quaint post offices, the modern postal clerk's role is dynamic, multifaceted, and vital to ensuring the smooth flow of communications and packages. This section will illuminate the responsibilities and tasks of these unsung heroes of the postal realm.

The Core of Clerk Operations

At its heart, a postal clerk ensures that mail, packages, and other postal products flow seamlessly from the point of origin to their intended destination. They stand as the backbone of back-end postal operations, bridging the gap between the sender, the postal system, and the recipient.

Mail and Package Sorting: The First Step

A postal clerk begins their day by sorting incoming mail and packages. They use advanced machinery and keen observation skills to categorize items based on size, destination, and type. It's a task that demands precision, for even a slight misstep can send a crucial letter or package astray.

Data Entry and Logging: The Digital Trace

In today's technologically driven era, manual operations intertwine with digital tasks. Postal clerks are responsible for entering data about mail and packages into specialized computer systems. This ensures tracking for customers and aids in internal inventory management and routing.

Rate and Postage Calculation: The Financial Aspects

Determining appropriate postage for varying mail types and packages is a critical task. Clerks use scales, rate charts, and computer systems to calculate and affix the correct postage, ensuring that items are neither overpaid nor underpaid.

Customer Service: The Human Touch

Beyond handling mail and packages, clerks often interact with customers, answering queries, guiding them on postal services, or helping them with paperwork for specialized services like money orders or international shipping. Their communication skills and deep understanding of postal operations are crucial to fostering trust and customer satisfaction.

Handling Special Items: The Delicate Dance

Certain items demand extra attention. Be it registered or certified mail, perishables, or fragile items, clerks ensure they receive the necessary care. They also manage the associated documentation and verify identities when required, maintaining the sanctity and security of the postal system.

Managing Returns and Undeliverable: The Loop Closure

Not all items find their way to their intended recipients. Clerks handle returns, manage undeliverable mail, and take steps to either redeliver or return them to the sender. This process can involve detective work, deciphering incorrect addresses, or liaising with carriers and customers.

Staying Abreast: Continuous Learning

The postal world is not static. With changing regulations, technologies, and service offerings, clerks continuously update their knowledge. Training sessions, workshops, and on-the-job learning ensure they remain at the forefront of postal operations.

Safety and Compliance: The Unwavering Commitment

Clerks adhere to stringent safety protocols, especially when handling potentially hazardous items. They're trained to recognize and manage such things following regulatory standards, ensuring their safety, colleagues, and the wider public.

Efficiency and Speed: The Clock Ticks

In the postal world, time is often of the essence. Clerks operate with a keen sense of urgency, ensuring that mail and packages move swiftly through the system. Their efficiency directly impacts delivery times, customer satisfaction, and the reputation of the postal service.

In the bustling corridors of postal facilities, amidst the hum of machinery and the perpetual movement of mail and packages, the postal clerk stands as a sentinel of order and efficiency. Their role, while often behind the scenes, is vital to the grand orchestra of postal operations.

By understanding the depth and breadth of their responsibilities, one gains a newfound appreciation for the intricate dance of back-end postal tasks. In a world of critical communication, the postal clerk ensures that every whisper, shout, and message finds its way home.

QUESTIONS AND ANSWERS

Delving into the intricate world of USPS examinations requires not just theoretical understanding but also practical insight. The Questions and Answers section is meticulously curated to provide readers with an in-depth look into the type of queries they might encounter, offering a chance to test their knowledge, identify areas of improvement, and solidify their understanding of the topics discussed. Each question has been designed with precision, drawing from real-world scenarios and concepts central to the postal service examinations.

EXAM 955 - MAINTENANCE AND ELECTRONICS

1. What is the primary focus of Exam 955?

Exam 955 centers on evaluating candidates' skills and knowledge in maintenance, electronics, and other technical proficiencies. It ensures potential USPS maintenance personnel have the expertise to manage and maintain equipment vital to postal operations.

2. Who typically takes Exam 955?

Those aspiring to assume USPS maintenance or electronic technician roles typically take Exam 955. The test measures their technical aptitude and readiness for the tasks they'll face in their roles.

3. How is the exam structured?

The exam encompasses multiple sections, each focusing on technical aspects such as electronics, spatial reasoning, and mechanical aptitude. This comprehensive structure ensures candidates are well-rounded in various maintenance domains.

4. Are there practical components to the exam?

Yes, Exam 955 includes scenarios and situations where candidates must practically apply their knowledge. This approach ensures they're theoretically sound and can handle real-world challenges.

5. Why is spatial reasoning tested in Exam 955?

Spatial reasoning is essential for maintenance and electronic tasks. It allows technicians to understand how components fit together, predict the outcomes of mechanical changes, and visualize solutions to complex problems.

6. Is knowledge of safety protocols assessed?

Absolutely. Safety is paramount in maintenance roles. Exam 955 evaluates a candidate's understanding of safe practices, ensuring they can carry out tasks without endangering themselves or others.

7. How do electronic principles play into the exam?

Understanding electronics principles is crucial, given the rise of automated machinery in postal operations. The exam tests candidates on basic electronics concepts, ensuring they can troubleshoot and repair electronic components.

8. Are candidates tested on software skills?

While the primary focus is on hardware, basic software skills are assessed, especially those related to equipment diagnostics and maintenance tools, this ensures a holistic understanding of modern maintenance tasks.

9. How significant is mechanical aptitude in Exam 955?

Mechanical aptitude is a cornerstone of the exam. It evaluates a candidate's innate ability to understand and work with machinery, which is vital for maintenance roles in USPS.

10. Is prior experience necessary to succeed?

While prior experience can be advantageous, Exam 955 is designed to test inherent skills and knowledge. Thus, even those new to the field but with a solid technical foundation can excel.

11. How does the USPS utilize the results of Exam 955?

USPS uses the results to identify and hire candidates best suited for maintenance roles. High scores often indicate a strong alignment with the technical demands of the position.

12. Is teamwork emphasized in the exam?

Indirectly, yes. While the exam tests individual knowledge, scenarios may involve situations where collaborative problem-solving is implied, reflecting real-world maintenance tasks.

13. What are the preparatory steps for Exam 955?

Candidates should review basic electronics principles, practice spatial reasoning exercises, and familiarize themselves with general mechanical concepts. Some also opt for formal training or courses.

14. How does Exam 955 relate to postal operations?

Maintenance and electronics are foundational to postal operations, ensuring machinery and systems run smoothly. Exam 955 identifies individuals who can uphold these standards, maintaining operational efficiency.

15. What is the significance of troubleshooting in the exam?

Troubleshooting is a primary skill for any technician. Exam 955 assesses a candidate's ability to diagnose issues and determine the best solutions, ensuring minimal downtime in real-world scenarios.

16. Does the exam cover modern machinery and tech?

Yes, the exam is continually updated to reflect current technologies and machinery used in USPS operations, ensuring candidates are prepared for contemporary challenges.

17. How do mechanical and electronic sections differ?

While both assess technical aptitude, the mechanical section focuses on machinery, gears, and physical components. In contrast, the electronics section delves into circuits, signals, and electronic theory.

18. Why is time management important for Exam 955?

Given the range of topics covered and the exam's comprehensive nature, managing time effectively ensures candidates can adequately address each section without feeling rushed.

19. Are candidates assessed on their ability to handle emergencies?

Yes. Real-world emergencies like equipment breakdowns are simulated to evaluate a candidate's ability to react promptly, make sound decisions, and prioritize safety.

20. How does Exam 955 align with industry standards?

The exam is designed in alignment with industry benchmarks for maintenance and electronics, ensuring that those who pass are not only fit for USPS but also meet broader industry norms.

21. Are there re-attempts for Exam 955?

Candidates who don't pass on their first attempt can re-apply and retake the exam, but there's usually a waiting period to ensure adequate preparation time.

22. How do candidates receive feedback post-exam?

After attempting Exam 955, candidates receive a score reflecting their performance. While detailed feedback isn't typically provided, the score clearly indicates areas of strength and those needing improvement.

23. What's the role of innovation in the exam?

While the exam tests foundational principles, innovative problem-solving is encouraged. Scenarios may require out-of-the-box thinking, mirroring real-world challenges where traditional solutions might not apply.

24. Are there any prerequisites for Exam 955?

There aren't strict prerequisites, but a background or education in mechanics, electronics, or a related field can benefit candidates attempting the exam.

25. How frequently is Exam 955 updated?

The frequency varies, but USPS ensures the exam remains relevant to current postal operations, technology, and machinery, incorporating updates as needed.

26. Are there specialized sections in the exam?

While the exam covers broad areas like electronics and mechanics, some subsections dive deeper into specific topics, ensuring a detailed assessment of every candidate's skills.

27. How does the exam accommodate advancements in tech?

As technology evolves, so does Exam 955. Newer technologies, machinery, and methods are incorporated into the exam structure, ensuring it remains current and applicable.

28. Why is the exam crucial for USPS operations?

Machinery and electronics are integral to USPS's efficiency. Exam 955 ensures that those tasked with maintaining this machinery possess the skills and knowledge to do so effectively.

29. Can candidates use reference materials during the exam?

Typically, Exam 955 is a closed book, emphasizing a candidate's inherent knowledge and skills without external aids.

30. Is there a practical hands-on component in Exam 955?

While the exam is mainly scenario-based and theoretical, the situations simulate practical challenges, gauging a candidate's readiness for hands-on tasks.

31. How does the exam test preventive maintenance skills?

Candidates encounter scenarios where they must identify early signs of wear and tear or potential breakdowns, assessing their preventive maintenance aptitude.

32. Are there ethical considerations in the exam?

Absolutely. While the primary focus is technical, the exam subtly evaluates a candidate's commitment to ethical practices, especially concerning safety and equipment handling.

33. How does the exam balance theory and application?

Exam 955 is meticulously crafted to test both theoretical knowledge and its practical application, ensuring candidates are well-rounded and can handle the demands of their role.

34. What are the key traits the exam seeks in candidates?

The exam seeks candidates with strong technical acumen, problem-solving skills, a commitment to safety, and the ability to adapt to evolving technologies.

35. How critical is precision in Exam 955?

Given the nature of maintenance tasks, precision is paramount. The exam emphasizes accuracy, ensuring candidates can perform tasks to exact standards.

36. How is a candidate's adaptability tested?

Scenarios in the exam often present unexpected challenges or shifts, gauging how well a candidate adapts to changing conditions or information.

37. Does the exam have a section on emerging technologies?

While foundational principles form the exam's core, emerging technologies are often included, reflecting the evolving nature of postal operations.

38. How does Exam 955 factor in environmental considerations?

With an increasing emphasis on sustainability, the exam incorporates scenarios where candidates must make decisions factoring in environmental impact and sustainable practices.

39. Are communication skills assessed in the exam?

Indirectly, yes. While technical skills are primary, the ability to communicate findings, issues, or solutions is implied in several scenarios, underlining the importance of clear communication in maintenance roles.

40. What support is available for candidates preparing for Exam 955?

Candidates can access various resources, including study guides, online forums, and training programs designed to bolster their preparation and chances of success in Exam 955.

EXAM 474 - MAIL CARRIER VEA

1. What is the main objective of Exam 474 - Mail Carrier VEA?

Exam 474 - Mail Carrier VEA primarily evaluates the potential aptitudes and characteristics of candidates aiming to serve as mail carriers within the USPS. It ensures that these individuals possess the necessary skills, temperament, and resilience to efficiently handle the challenges they might face during their daily routes, from accurate deliveries to prompt customer interactions.

2. Who is the ideal candidate for this exam?

The ideal candidate for Exam 474 is someone who demonstrates punctuality, strong organizational skills, keen attention to detail, and the ability to work independently. Physical stamina and good interpersonal skills are also essential since mail carriers often interact with customers and cover vast routes.

3. What sets Exam 474 apart from other postal exams?

While all postal exams aim to assess the readiness of candidates for various USPS roles, Exam 474 explicitly targets the competencies and attributes necessary for mail carriers. This involves testing route efficiency, understanding postal regulations, and ensuring customer satisfaction.

4. How does the exam evaluate route management skills?

Exam 474 presents candidates with scenarios that simulate challenges faced during mail delivery routes. It assesses how well candidates prioritize tasks, strategize ways for efficiency, and handle unexpected interruptions or changes.

5. Why is customer service an integral component of Exam 474?

Mail carriers frequently interact with customers during their routes. Exam 474 emphasizes the importance of maintaining positive customer relations, addressing concerns, and ensuring that mail recipients are satisfied with the service.

6. How does the exam cater to modern mail delivery challenges?

The USPS continually evolves to accommodate technological advancements and changing customer needs. Exam 474 incorporates scenarios that reflect these modern challenges, such as managing package deliveries from online shopping or using electronic devices for delivery tracking.

7. Are candidates tested on their knowledge of USPS regulations?

Yes, mail carriers need to be conversant with USPS regulations to ensure the integrity and efficiency of mail delivery. Exam 474 evaluates this knowledge, providing pages that can uphold the standards set by the USPS.

8. How does physical stamina play into the exam?

While the exam doesn't test physical stamina directly, scenarios might allude to the rigors of the job, such as walking long distances, managing heavy packages, or handling adverse weather conditions. This indirectly assesses the candidate's understanding of the role's physical demands.

9. Is there an emphasis on problem-solving in the exam?

Absolutely. Mail carriers often face unexpected challenges, from incorrect addresses to delivery disputes. Exam 474 assesses a candidate's ability to think independently and find practical solutions promptly.

10. How do candidates prepare for Exam 474?

Preparation involves familiarizing oneself with USPS regulations, understanding route management strategies, honing customer service skills, and studying potential scenarios they might encounter. Many candidates also access study guides or join preparatory courses tailored for Exam 474.

11. Why is time management an essential aspect of Exam 474?

With mail carriers working within specific delivery windows, managing time efficiently is crucial. Exam 474 evaluates how candidates allocate their time, prioritize deliveries, and streamline their routes for maximum efficiency.

12. How do safety and ethical considerations feature in the exam?

The USPS places immense importance on the safety and ethical handling of mail. Exam 474 tests candidates on safety protocols, from handling packages to ensuring personal safety during deliveries. Ethical considerations, like respecting customer privacy and ensuring mail integrity, are also assessed.

13. Are there sections in Exam 474 that deal with mail categorization?

Yes, understanding mail categorization is vital for efficient sorting and delivery. Exam 474 evaluates the candidates' proficiency in identifying and organizing various mail types, ensuring that the suitable parcels reach the intended recipients.

14. How does the exam prepare candidates for inclement weather challenges?

Mail carriers operate in all weather conditions. Exam 474 might present scenarios where candidates must strategize deliveries during rain, snow, or extreme heat, emphasizing the role's demanding nature and the need for adaptability.

15. Is there a focus on package handling skills?

Indeed, with the surge in online shopping, mail carriers handle a higher volume of packages than ever before. Exam 474 evaluates how efficiently candidates manage, organize, and deliver these packages without delays or damage.

16. Are interpersonal skills vital for Exam 474?

Undoubtedly. While the technical aspects of mail delivery are crucial, the human element is equally important. Mail carriers often serve as the face of USPS for many customers, making interpersonal skills essential for maintaining the USPS's reputation.

17. How does the exam accommodate changes in mail delivery technology?

The USPS frequently adopts new technologies to streamline operations. Exam 474 is updated to reflect these changes, ensuring candidates are familiar with modern tools, from electronic scanners to route optimization software.

18. How important is attention to detail for a mail carrier?

It's paramount. A minor oversight can lead to undelivered or misplaced mail, causing inconvenience for customers. Exam 474 tests candidates' meticulousness in ensuring every mail piece reaches its correct destination.

19. How does the exam gauge stress management?

Being a mail carrier can be stressful, from managing vast routes to handling customer complaints. Exam 474 presents high-pressure scenarios to assess how candidates cope with stress and deliver efficient service.

20. Why is familiarity with local areas emphasized in the exam?

Knowing the local area streamlines deliveries. Candidates familiar with local landmarks, streets, and neighborhoods can optimize their routes better, ensuring timely and accurate deliveries.

21. Does Exam 474 test the candidate's ability to handle demanding customers?

Yes. Mail carriers sometimes encounter disgruntled customers or delivery disputes. The exam evaluates how candidates address these situations, emphasizing patience, professionalism, and practical resolution skills.

22. How does the USPS ensure that Exam 474 remains relevant?

The USPS continually reviews and updates the exam content, incorporating feedback from experienced mail carriers and adjusting to technological advancements and evolving customer needs.

23. Is teamwork a component of the exam?

While mail carriers work independently, teamwork is occasionally needed, especially during the sorting process or peak delivery times. Exam 474 touches upon this aspect, emphasizing the importance of collaboration in specific scenarios.

24. Are there any sections on international mail in Exam 474?

Given the global nature of mail delivery, international mail considerations are a component of Exam 474. Candidates are assessed on their understanding of international mail regulations, categories, and delivery protocols.

25. How does the exam prepare candidates for holiday season deliveries?

The holiday season is a peak period for mail carriers. Exam 474 presents scenarios simulating the heightened demands of this season, testing candidates' ability to manage increased workloads efficiently.

26. Does the exam factor in evolving customer expectations?

Absolutely. Customer expectations regarding timely and accurate deliveries have increased in the digital age. Exam 474 ensures candidates are prepared to meet these evolving demands.

27. How do candidates handle misdeliveries in the exam scenarios?

Misdeliveries are a concern for any mail carrier. The exam evaluates how candidates address such situations, from tracing the misplaced mail to ensuring it reaches the intended recipient without delays.

28. Is there a focus on confidentiality and mail security?

Yes. Maintaining mail confidentiality and ensuring its security is paramount. Exam 474 tests candidates' understanding of these principles, emphasizing the importance of trust in the mail carrier role.

29. How do candidates demonstrate their commitment to the USPS's mission in the exam?

Through various scenarios, candidates showcase their dedication to upholding the USPS's values, ensuring efficient mail delivery, and maintaining customer trust and satisfaction.

30. Are there any technological tools mail carriers use that feature in Exam 474?

The exam incorporates scenarios where candidates might use technological tools, from hand-held scanners for tracking deliveries to software tools for route optimization.

31. How does the exam emphasize the physical aspects of the mail carrier role?

Scenarios in Exam 474 allude to the role's physical demands, from walking several miles a day to lifting heavy packages, ensuring candidates understand the rigors they might face.

32. How critical are punctuality and reliability in the exam?

These are cornerstones of the mail carrier role. Exam 474 evaluates candidates' commitment to these principles, ensuring mail reaches recipients promptly and consistently.

33. Does the exam prepare candidates for urban and rural mail deliveries?

Yes, scenarios in the exam simulate challenges specific to both urban and rural settings, from navigating bustling city streets to understanding the nuances of delivering mail in remote areas.

34. How do candidates demonstrate multitasking in the exam?

With various tasks, from sorting to delivery, multitasking is essential. Exam 474 evaluates this skill by presenting scenarios where candidates must juggle multiple responsibilities efficiently.

35. Are there any sections on special mail categories like Priority Mail or Certified Mail?

Special mail categories are integral to USPS operations. Exam 474 tests candidates' understanding of these categories, ensuring they can handle and deliver such mail according to USPS standards.

36. How does Exam 474 factor in evolving postal regulations?

As postal regulations evolve, the content of Exam 474 is updated to reflect these changes, ensuring candidates are constantly tested on the most recent and relevant information.

37. How does the exam test organizational skills?

Organizing mail, optimizing routes, and prioritizing deliveries are core components of the mail carrier role. Exam 474 evaluates these organizational skills through various scenarios, ensuring candidates can streamline their daily operations.

38. How do candidates handle package disputes in the exam?

The exam presents scenarios where recipients might dispute deliveries or claim non-receipt. Candidates are assessed on their resolution skills, emphasizing effective communication and problem-solving.

39. Are there any sections on hazardous materials in the mail?

Handling and recognizing hazardous materials is crucial for safety. Exam 474 touches upon this, evaluating candidates' knowledge of safety protocols and ability to identify potentially dangerous mail.

40. How do mail carriers handle peak delivery times, and how is this reflected in the exam?

Peak delivery times, like during the holiday season, require extra diligence. Exam 474 presents scenarios simulating these peak periods, assessing candidates' capacity to manage increased workloads and maintain high delivery standards.

EXAM 475 - MAIL HANDLER VEA

1. What is the primary purpose of Exam 475 - Mail Handler VEA?

The primary aim of Exam 475 is to assess the qualifications and competencies of candidates aspiring to be mail handlers within the USPS. These individuals play a pivotal role in the mail processing stages, ensuring accuracy, efficiency, and timeliness.

2. How does the role of a mail handler differ from that of a mail carrier?

While mail carriers are responsible for delivering mail and packages to recipients, mail handlers focus on the internal operations of USPS facilities. They categorize, sort, and dispatch mail, ensuring it's ready for delivery by mail carriers.

3. What essential skills are assessed in Exam 475?

Exam 475 evaluates a variety of competencies, including organizational skills, attention to detail, the ability to handle large volumes of mail efficiently, understanding of USPS regulations, and proficiency in using mail processing equipment.

4. Why is speed a crucial aspect of the mail handler role?

Given the vast amount of mail processed daily, speed is of the essence. A mail handler must work swiftly without compromising accuracy to ensure timely delivery and maintain the USPS's service standards.

5. How does Exam 475 test the candidates' understanding of mail categorization?

Candidates encounter scenarios and tasks requiring them to sort and categorize various mail types, from letters to parcels, ensuring they comprehend the different categories and can process them accordingly.

6. Is knowledge of machinery and equipment essential for Exam 475?

Absolutely. Mail handlers often use automated machines to expedite the sorting process. Exam 475 assesses candidates' familiarity with such equipment and proficiency in handling machine-related issues.

7. How does the exam evaluate adaptability in high-pressure scenarios?

Exam 475 presents candidates with situations simulating peak mail periods or unexpected influxes. It gauges how candidates adapt, strategize, and maintain efficiency in demanding circumstances.

8. Why is teamwork emphasized in the mail handler role?

Mail handlers often work in teams, collaborating to ensure smooth operations. Exam 475 assesses the ability of candidates to work harmoniously with colleagues, providing collective efficiency and a conducive work environment.

9. How does Exam 475 prepare candidates for the role's physical demands?

Mail handlers might lift heavy parcels or be on their feet for extended periods. Scenarios in Exam 475 allude to these physical demands, ensuring candidates understand and are prepared for the rigors of the role.

10. Why is safety an integral component of the exam?

In USPS facilities, the safety of both personnel and mail is paramount. Exam 475 evaluates candidates' awareness of safety protocols and commitment to ensuring a hazard-free workspace.

11. How do mail handlers ensure the integrity of mail?

Exam 475 tests candidates' understanding of maintaining mail integrity. This involves ensuring mail is kept intact during the sorting and dispatching.

12. Are there sections in Exam 475 that address particular mail types, such as registered or insured mail?

Yes. Handling special mail categories requires extra diligence. Exam 475 assesses candidates' knowledge and handling of these specific mail types, emphasizing the importance of their secure and accurate processing.

13. How do mail handlers contribute to the overall efficiency of the USPS?

Mail handlers play a pivotal role in ensuring the mail is sorted and dispatched timely and accurately. Exam 475 underscores this role, testing candidates' ability to contribute effectively to the USPS's overarching efficiency.

14. What challenges might mail handlers face, and how does Exam 475 address these?

From machine malfunctions to deciphering illegible addresses, mail handlers encounter various challenges. Exam 475 simulates such situations, assessing candidates' problem-solving skills and adaptability.

15. How do candidates demonstrate their multitasking abilities in the exam?

Multitasking is essential given the myriad tasks under a mail handler's purview. Exam 475 evaluates this skill by presenting scenarios requiring candidates to juggle multiple responsibilities efficiently.

16. Why is a thorough understanding of postal regulations vital for mail handlers?

Mail handlers ensure the mail aligns with USPS regulations before dispatching. Exam 475 tests candidates' knowledge of these regulations, ensuring they can uphold the USPS's standards.

17. How does the exam emphasize the importance of accuracy?

Accuracy is paramount to ensure timely deliveries and losses. Exam 475 presents tasks and scenarios that assess a candidate's meticulousness, emphasizing the importance of error-free mail processing.

18. How do mail handlers handle confidential or sensitive mail?

Given the importance of privacy, mail handlers must ensure the confidentiality of sensitive mail. Exam 475 evaluates candidates' commitment to this principle and their understanding of related USPS regulations.

19. Are there any technological aspects addressed in Exam 475?

Certainly. With the USPS adopting modern technologies for mail processing, Exam 475 tests candidates' familiarity with digital tools and systems used in mail handling operations.

20. How does Exam 475 prepare candidates for varying work shifts?

Mail handlers might work in different shifts, including nights. Exam 475 scenarios address the challenges and adaptations required for such changes, ensuring candidates are prepared for this aspect of the role.

21. How do mail handlers prioritize mail during peak periods?

During peak times, prioritization becomes crucial. Exam 475 evaluates how candidates prioritize mail types, especially time-sensitive ones, to ensure timely processing and dispatch.

22. Are there any sections in Exam 475 addressing hazardous materials?

Absolutely. Recognizing and safely handling hazardous materials is vital. Exam 475 tests candidates' ability to identify and manage materials following USPS guidelines.

23. How do mail handlers collaborate with other USPS roles?

Mail handlers work in tandem with mail carriers, clerks, and other USPS personnel. Exam 475 assesses candidates' understanding of this interdepartmental collaboration, ensuring they can contribute to a seamless workflow.

24. What role do mail handlers play in addressing customer complaints?

While they might not interact directly with customers, mail handlers address internal issues leading to customer complaints. Exam 475 evaluates how candidates handle and rectify such issues.

25. How does the exam factor in evolving industry standards?

Exam 475 content is updated as postal standards evolve to reflect these changes, ensuring candidates are constantly tested on the most recent and relevant information.

26. How does Exam 475 assess organizational skills?

Organizing mail efficiently is a core mail handler responsibility. Exam 475 evaluates these skills through tasks and scenarios that test candidates' ability to streamline mail operations.

27. How critical is attention to detail for mail handlers?

A keen eye for detail is essential, given the importance of accurate mail processing. Exam 475 emphasizes this quality, testing candidates' ability to detect and rectify anomalies.

28. How do mail handlers manage lost or misplaced mail?

Managing misplaced mail is a challenging aspect of the role. Exam 475 presents scenarios where candidates must trace and recover such mail, ensuring it eventually reaches its intended destination.

29. How does the exam address handling oversized or irregular mail?

Specific mail needs to fit standard categorizations. Exam 475 tests candidates' ability to process such irregular items, ensuring they're handled carefully and dispatched correctly.

30. Why is continuous learning emphasized for mail handlers?

With evolving technologies and regulations, mail handlers must stay updated. Exam 475 underscores the importance of continuous learning, assessing candidates' willingness to adapt and evolve.

31. How do mail handlers contribute to sustainability and eco-friendly practices?

In line with global sustainability trends, USPS has eco-friendly initiatives. Exam 475 touches upon this, assessing how candidates can contribute to these initiatives in their role.

32. How do candidates handle package disputes internally?

While not directly dealing with customers, mail handlers play a role in resolving internal package disputes. Exam 475 evaluates this aspect, emphasizing effective communication and resolution skills.

33. How does Exam 475 address the security aspects of the mail handler role?

Mail security is paramount. Exam 475 tests candidates' understanding of security protocols, ensuring they can maintain a secure environment for mail processing.

34. Why is punctuality emphasized for mail handlers?

Timely mail processing is crucial for the USPS's efficiency. Exam 475 evaluates candidates' commitment to punctuality, ensuring they can meet processing deadlines consistently.

35. How do mail handlers address the wear and tear of machinery?

Regular maintenance of mail processing machinery is essential. Exam 475 assesses candidates' understanding of machinery maintenance and their ability to address minor malfunctions.

36. How do mail handlers ensure smooth operations during staff shortages?

Adapting to staff shortages and ensuring no lapse in service is crucial. Exam 475 presents scenarios simulating such situations, assessing how candidates adapt and maintain efficiency.

37. What role do mail handlers play in inventory management?

While not a primary role, mail handlers might assist in inventory tasks. Exam 475 touches upon this aspect, testing candidates' understanding of inventory protocols within USPS facilities.

38. How do mail handlers ensure they're updated on USPS guidelines?

Staying updated is essential for adherence to USPS standards. Exam 475 evaluates candidates' commitment to continuous learning and strategies to keep abreast of the latest USPS guidelines.

39. How does Exam 475 address potential conflicts in the workplace?

Workplace harmony is vital for efficiency. Exam 475 presents scenarios where candidates might encounter conflicts, assessing their conflict resolution skills and commitment to a harmonious work environment.

40. Why is customer satisfaction indirectly linked to the role of mail handlers?

Though mail handlers don't interact with customers directly, their efficiency affects delivery times and accuracy, impacting customer satisfaction. Exam 475 underscores their indirect yet pivotal role in ensuring customer satisfaction.

EXAM 477 - CUSTOMER SERVICE/CLERK VEA

1. What is the main objective of Exam 477 - Customer Service/Clerk VEA?

Exam 477 aims to evaluate the competencies and qualifications of individuals seeking clerk or customer service roles within the USPS, ensuring they can offer high-quality service and manage postal operations effectively.

2. How crucial is customer interaction in this role?

Customer interaction forms the crux of the clerk or customer service role. The exam gauges a candidate's communication skills, patience, and ability to handle varied customer queries and concerns.

3. What aspects of postal operations are emphasized in Exam 477?

Exam 477 focuses on various postal operations, from sorting mail and managing postal transactions to understanding postal rates and regulations and using postal software efficiently.

4. How does the exam test the candidate's ability to handle demanding customers?

Scenarios in the exam simulate challenging customer situations. Candidates' responses assess their ability to remain calm, provide accurate information, and resolve issues diplomatically.

5. Why is knowledge of postal rates and services essential?

Given frequent customer interactions regarding mailing options, rates, and services, Exam 477 evaluates a candidate's comprehensive understanding of these areas, ensuring accurate information dissemination.

6. How does Exam 477 assess multitasking abilities?

Clerks often juggle multiple responsibilities simultaneously. The exam presents scenarios that require candidates to handle multiple tasks efficiently, gauging their multitasking proficiency.

7. In what way does the exam emphasize clerical accuracy?

Accuracy is paramount, especially in postal transactions and record-keeping. Exam 477 evaluates a candidate's meticulousness and commitment to error-free operations.

8. How is the candidate's familiarity with postal software evaluated?

Given the digital tools used in USPS operations, the exam assesses a candidate's proficiency with such software, ensuring they can process transactions and manage records efficiently.

9. What role does a clerk play in addressing customer complaints?

Clerks often serve as the first point of contact for customer grievances. Exam 477 tests a candidate's problem-solving skills and ability to resolve issues effectively, ensuring customer satisfaction.

10. How does the exam evaluate the ability to handle high-pressure situations?

Exam 477 simulates peak hours and challenging situations, assessing how candidates prioritize tasks, manage time, and maintain composure.

11. How do clerks collaborate with other USPS roles?

Clerks work alongside mail carriers, handlers, and other USPS personnel. The exam evaluates the understanding of this collaborative aspect, ensuring smooth inter-departmental operations.

12. What significance does product knowledge have for this role?

From stamps to packaging solutions, clerks must be well-versed with USPS products. Exam 477 assesses this knowledge, ensuring candidates can advise customers effectively.

13. How does the exam address the handling of financial transactions?

Clerks handle sales and postal transactions. Exam 477 evaluates candidates' accuracy in handling money, processing payments, and maintaining transaction records.

14. What role does feedback play in a clerk's responsibilities?

Clerks gather feedback to improve USPS services. Exam 477 tests candidates' ability to effectively solicit, understand, and relay feedback to higher-ups.

15. How does Exam 477 prepare candidates for varying work shifts?

USPS clerks might work different shifts, including weekends. The exam presents scenarios related to these shifts, assessing candidates' adaptability and preparedness.

16. How do clerks ensure customer data privacy?

Given the sensitive nature of postal information, maintaining privacy is paramount. Exam 477 evaluates candidates' commitment to data protection and adherence to USPS's privacy standards.

17. How is the candidate's knowledge of international shipping assessed?

With global shipping being an essential USPS service, the exam tests candidates' understanding of international rates, regulations, and procedures.

18. Why is continuous learning emphasized in the clerk role?

The postal industry evolves continually. Exam 477 underscores the importance of staying updated on products, services, and regulations, ensuring candidates are always informed.

19. How do clerks manage stock and inventory?

From stamps to packaging materials, clerks manage inventory. Exam 477 evaluates candidates' understanding of inventory management and restocking procedures.

20. How do clerks handle undeliverable or returned mail?

Handling such mail requires care and accuracy. The exam tests candidates' proficiency in processing undeliverable items, ensuring they're redirected or returned correctly.

21. Why is a proactive approach essential for clerks?

Being proactive ensures customer queries are addressed before they escalate. Exam 477 evaluates candidates' ability to anticipate issues and offer timely solutions.

22. How do clerks contribute to USPS's sustainability initiatives?

Awareness of eco-friendly practices and products is essential. Exam 477 tests candidates' knowledge of USPS's green initiatives and their ability to promote them to customers.

23. What role does technology play in the clerk's responsibilities?

From postal software to digital payment systems, technology is pivotal. Exam 477 assesses candidates' proficiency in using and troubleshooting these technologies.

24. How do clerks handle discrepancies in transactions?

Addressing discrepancies promptly and accurately is crucial. Exam 477 evaluates candidates' ability to spot, rectify, and prevent transactional errors.

25. How do clerks assist customers in choosing the right postal solutions?

By understanding customer needs and being knowledgeable about USPS services. Exam 477 tests candidates' advisory skills, ensuring they can guide customers effectively.

26. How do clerks maintain the cleanliness and organization of their workspace?

A tidy workspace ensures efficiency. Exam 477 evaluates candidates' commitment to maintaining an organized, hazard-free environment.

27. How does Exam 477 address potential workplace conflicts?

The exam simulates situations where candidates might face conflicts, testing their diplomatic conflict-resolution skills and team collaboration.

28. How do clerks ensure accuracy in weight and postage?

Using the right tools and meticulousness is critical. Exam 477 assesses candidates' precision in weighing items and calculating correct postage.

29. How do clerks handle special service requests, like money orders?

Such services require additional care and knowledge. Exam 477 evaluates candidates' proficiency in processing special requests, ensuring customer satisfaction.

30. Why is cultural sensitivity important for clerks?

Given the diverse clientele, understanding and respecting cultural nuances is crucial. Exam 477 tests candidates' cultural awareness and ability to respectfully serve all customers.

31. How do clerks handle language barriers?

Effective communication is vital. The exam assesses candidates' strategies for addressing language barriers, from using translation tools to seeking assistance.

32. How do clerks contribute to peak holiday season operations?

The holiday season sees a surge in postal demands. Exam 477 evaluates candidates' ability to manage this increased workload efficiently, ensuring timely deliveries and satisfied customers.

33. How do clerks stay updated on USPS promotions and offers?

Regular training and updates are crucial. Exam 477 tests candidates' commitment to staying informed and ability to relay the latest promotions to customers.

34. How do clerks manage long customer queues?

Efficiency and patience are critical. Exam 477 assesses how candidates handle pressure, prioritize tasks, and ensure smooth customer interactions, even during peak times.

35. What role does feedback play in improving clerk operations?

Feedback provides insights into areas of improvement. Exam 477 evaluates candidates' receptiveness to feedback and their ability to implement changes for enhanced operations.

36. How do clerks ensure the safety and security of the mail?

By adhering to USPS's strict security guidelines. Exam 477 tests candidates' commitment to these protocols, ensuring the mail's safety and integrity.

37. How do clerks process payments for various services?

Using USPS's digital systems and maintaining accuracy is essential. Exam 477 evaluates candidates' proficiency in processing diverse payment types and maintaining transaction records.

38. Why is adaptability emphasized for clerks?

Given the dynamic nature of the postal environment, being adaptable ensures efficiency. Exam 477 tests candidates' ability to adapt to changing circumstances and evolving postal operations.

39. How do clerks manage personal breaks without affecting operations?

Efficient time management ensures seamless operations. Exam 477 assesses candidates' ability to manage personal breaks, providing minimal disruptions to service.

40. How do clerks contribute to the overall success of a USPS facility?

By offering excellent customer service, efficient operations, and collaboration. Exam 477 evaluates candidates' holistic contribution to a USPS facility's success, ensuring they're assets to the organization.

PRACTICE TEST

Practice, as they say, makes perfect. The Practice Tests section offers aspirants a simulated experience of the actual USPS examinations. Crafted with utmost care, these tests mirror the actual exams' format, difficulty, and depth, enabling candidates to gauge their preparedness, hone their skills, and build confidence. It's an invaluable resource for those seeking to experience the examination ambiance before the test day, ensuring they are well-equipped to tackle any challenge.

EXAM 955 - MAINTENANCE AND ELECTRONICS

1. **Question:** In a primary electric circuit, what causes electrons to move?

   A) Capacitor

   B) Transistor

   C) Voltage

   D) Inductor

2. **Question:** Which law states that the current through a conductor between two points is directly proportional to the voltage across the two points?

   A) Joule's Law

   B) Newton's Law

   C) Coulomb's Law

   D) Ohm's Law

3. **Question:** What happens when the P-side is connected to the negative terminal in a diode?

   A) Forward Bias

   B) Reverse Bias

   C) No Bias

   D) Neutral Bias

4. **Question:** Which of the following electronic components stores energy in an electric field?

   A) Resistor

   B) Inductor

   C) Diode

   D) Capacitor

5. **Question:** Which device converts mechanical energy into electrical energy?

   A) Motor

   B) Generator

   C) Transformer

   D) Resistor

6. **Question:** Which of the following best describes a transistor?

   A) A mechanical switch

   B) A type of resistor

   C) A current-controlled current source

   D) A magnetic storage device

7. **Question:** What is the primary purpose of a transformer?

   A) Convert DC to AC

   B) Increase or decrease voltage levels

   C) Store electrical energy

   D) Control electrical resistance

8. **Question:** Which component is primarily used for frequency filtration in circuits?

   A) Diode

   B) Transformer

   C) Resistor

   D) Capacitor

9. **Question:** In a series circuit, how does current flow through components?

   A) Varies based on the resistance

   B) Same through all components

   C) Inversely proportional to voltage

   D) It doesn't flow

10. **Question:** What does the color banding on a resistor indicate?

    A) Its inductance

    B) Its capacitance

    C) Its operational frequency

    D) Its resistance value

11. Question: Which component blocks DC but allows AC to pass through?

    A) Diode

    B) Resistor

    C) Capacitor

    D) Transformer

12. Question: How does increasing the temperature generally affect a semiconductor's conductivity?

    A) Increases

    B) Decreases

    C) Remains constant

    D) Turns infinite

13. Question: What is the purpose of a rectifier in an electronic circuit?

    A) Amplify signals

    B) Convert AC to DC

    C) Store electrical energy

    D) Modulate frequency

14. Question: In which type of circuit are components connected across common points or junctions?

    A) Series

    B) Parallel

    C) Integrated

    D) Modulated

15. Question: Which device is specifically designed to amplify electrical signals?

    A) Transformer

    B) Resistor

    C) Capacitor

    D) Transistor

16. Question: What is the unit of capacitance?

    A) Henry

    B) Ohm

    C) Farad

    D) Coulomb

17. Question: In digital electronics, which logic gate provides an output only when all its inputs are low?

A) OR

B) AND

C) NAND

D) NOR

18. Question: Which law states that the current through a conductor is directly proportional to the voltage across it and inversely proportional to its resistance?

A) Joule's Law

B) Faraday's Law

C) Ohm's Law

D) Kirchhoff's Law

19. Question: What is the primary function of a diode in electronics?

A) Resist current flow

B) Amplify current

C) Allow current flow in one direction

D) Store energy

20. Question: Which type of capacitor is polarized and must be connected with the correct polarity in a circuit?

A) Ceramic

B) Mylar

C) Electrolytic

D) Polystyrene

21. Question: A sudden, transient, and short-duration surge in voltage in an electrical circuit is termed a?

A) Brownout

B) Blackout

C) Spike

D) Noise

22. Question: In a logic circuit, which gate produces a low output only when both inputs are high?

A) OR

B) AND

C) NAND

D) XOR

23. Question: Which component is essential for tuning radio frequencies?

   A) Diode

   B) Resistor

   C) Variable capacitor

   D) Transformer

24. Question: Which phenomenon describes the opposition to the change of electric current in a circuit?

   A) Resistance

   B) Capacitance

   C) Inductance

   D) Conductance

25. Question: In a transformer, what component helps transfer energy from the primary to the secondary winding?

   A) Diode

   B) Core

   C) Capacitor

   D) Resistor

26. Question: Which of the following devices converts electrical energy into mechanical energy?

   A) Generator

   B) Motor

   C) Resistor

   D) Capacitor

27. Question: Which modulation type varies the carrier wave frequency by the signal?

   A) Amplitude Modulation (AM)

   B) Pulse Code Modulation (PCM)

   C) Frequency Modulation (FM)

   D) Phase Modulation (PM)

28. Question: What function does a rectifier serve in electronic circuits?

   A) Amplify signals

   B) Store energy

   C) Convert AC to DC

   D) Increase resistance

29. Question: In the context of semiconductors, what does 'PNP' denote in a bipolar junction transistor?

   A) Two p-type materials separated by an n-type

   B) Two n-type materials separated by a p-type

   C) An integrated mixture of positive and negative materials

   D) A double-layered n-type material

30. Question: Which electronic component functions as a two-terminal, non-linear resistor?

   A) Diode

   B) Varistor

   C) Capacitor

   D) Transformer

31. Question: How is the 'Q-factor' relevant in electronics?

   A) It measures the quality of resonance in a circuit.

   B) It calculates the quantity of charge in a capacitor.

   C) It denotes the quantum efficiency of a device.

   D) It represents the quickness of a digital signal.

32. Question: Which circuit component is employed to store electric charge temporarily?

   A) Resistor

   B) Inductor

   C) Diode

   D) Capacitor

33. Question: Which gate gives a high output in digital electronics when its two inputs are different?

   A) AND

   B) OR

   C) NOR

   D) XOR

34. Question: What kind of electronic component relies on the tunneling effect?

   A) Transformer

   B) Tunnel Diode

   C) Resistor

   D) Capacitor

35. Question: What is the primary purpose of a heat sink in electronic circuits?

A) Generate heat

B) Store electrical energy

C) Dissipate heat

D) Measure temperature

36. Question: Which law states that the voltage across a conductor is proportional to the current passing through it?

A) Joule's Law

B) Faraday's Law

C) Ohm's Law

D) Kirchhoff's Law

37. Question: What term describes the rate at which work is done, or energy is transformed in an electrical system?

A) Resistance

B) Power

C) Current

D) Voltage

38. Question: Which electronic component is designed to amplify the strength of a signal?

A) Oscillator

B) Amplifier

C) Modulator

D) Mixer

39. Question: In which component is the piezoelectric effect employed?

A) Resistor

B) Diode

C) Capacitor

D) Quartz Crystal

40. Question: Which component uses a p-n junction to emit light when current flows through it?

A) Light Emitting Resistor

B) Incandescent Bulb

C) Light Emitting Diode (LED)

D) Fluorescent Tube

41. Question: What is the primary function of a relay in electronic circuits?

   A) Amplify signals

   B) Store energy

   C) Convert frequencies

   D) Switch circuits

42. Question: Which of the following is NOT a type of transistor?

   A) BJT

   B) FET

   C) MOSFET

   D) QED

43. Question: How many stable states do a bistable multivibrator have in a digital system?

   A) One

   B) Two

   C) Three

   D) Four

EXAM 474 - MAIL CARRIER VEA

1. **Question:** What is the primary duty of a Mail Carrier?

   A) Sorting mail at the post office

   B) Delivering mail to recipients

   C) Packing boxes for shipment

   D) Driving the postmaster to meetings

2. **Question:** How often do Mail Carriers typically deliver mail?

   A) Weekly

   B) Daily

   C) Monthly

   D) Yearly

3. **Question:** Which tool helps Mail Carriers keep mail organized during delivery?

   A) Barcode scanner

   B) Mail satchel

   C) Stamps

   D) Cash register

4. **Question:** What weather conditions can be a challenge for Mail Carriers?

   A) Clear skies

   B) Snow

   C) Indoor rain

   D) None

5. **Question:** Which of the following is a safety precaution Mail Carriers must take?

   A) Avoiding animals like dogs

   B) Eating mail

   C) Ignoring traffic signals

   D) Carrying flammable liquids

6. **Question:** How should Mail Carriers handle undeliverable mail?

   A) Leave it on the doorstep

   B) Return it to the post office

   C) Dispose of it

   D) Keep it

7. **Question:** What is one challenge Mail Carriers face during the holiday season?

   A) Less mail to deliver

   B) Shorter working hours

   C) Increased mail volume

   D) More vacations

8. **Question:** Which vehicle is most commonly used by Mail Carriers in suburban areas?

   A) Motorcycles

   B) Bicycles

   C) LLVs (Long Life Vehicles)

   D) Helicopters

9. **Question:** Which type of mail requires a recipient's signature upon delivery?

   A) First-class mail

   B) Catalogs

   C) Magazines

   D) Certified mail

10. **Question:** What technology has improved efficiency for Mail Carriers during their routes?

    A) GPS devices

    B) Vintage compasses

    C) Paper maps

    D) Abacus

11. **Question:** Who sets the guidelines and regulations for mail delivery?

    A) The President

    B) Local municipalities

    C) The postmaster general

    D) USPS

12. **Question:** In what scenario might a Mail Carrier hold mail?

    A) If they don't feel like delivering

    B) If the recipient is on vacation

    C) On sunny days

    D) None of the above

13. Question: How do Mail Carriers handle fragile items?

   A) Toss them into the back of the vehicle

   B) Deliver them with extra care

   C) Open them to check if they're genuinely fragile

   D) Avoid them

14. Question: What's a critical skill for a Mail Carrier?

   A) Ability to decode encrypted messages

   B) A passion for stamp collecting

   C) Knowledge of local delivery routes

   D) Culinary expertise

15. Question: What equipment is essential for a Mail Carrier on foot?

   A) A pair of roller skates

   B) A comfortable pair of shoes

   C) A helmet

   D) Night vision goggles

16. Question: What happens if a recipient is away from home to receive a package?

   A) The Mail Carrier leaves a notice

   B) The Mail Carrier waits at the door

   C) The package is returned to the sender immediately

   D) The package is left with a neighbor without notice

17. Question: How do Mail Carriers ensure mail and packages stay dry in the rain?

   A) By using magic

   B) By using protective coverings and gear

   C) By avoiding mail delivery on rainy days

   D) They don't; mail gets wet

18. Question: Which of these is a potential hazard for Mail Carriers?

   A) Birds

   B) Rainbows

   C) Clouds

   D) Busy intersections

19. **Question:** Which service involves tracking and delivery notifications for recipients?

   A) Media mail

   B) Priority Mail Express

   C) Book shipments

   D) First-class letters

20. **Question:** Why is it essential for Mail Carriers to be familiar with their routes?

   A) So they can sightsee

   B) To ensure timely delivery

   C) To avoid meeting residents

   D) None of the above

21. **Question:** What is the primary responsibility of a Mail Carrier?

   A) Package wrapping

   B) Mail sorting only

   C) Ensuring timely delivery of mail and packages

   D) Driving the mail truck only

22. **Question:** Which of the following is NOT a physical requirement for a Mail Carrier?

   A) Ability to lift heavy packages

   B) Knowledge of postal regulations

   C) Stamina for walking long distances

   D) Good eyesight

23. **Question:** What should a Mail Carrier do when faced with an aggressive dog?

   A) Engage with the dog playfully

   B) Offer food

   C) Try to run away as fast as possible

   D) Avoid eye contact and back away slowly

24. **Question:** How do Mail Carriers typically start their day?

   A) By delivering emails immediately

   B) With a team meeting

   C) Sorting and organizing mail for delivery

   D) By refueling their vehicles

25. Question: In inclement weather, what tool can aid Mail Carriers in delivering mail?

    A) GPS

    B) Umbrella

    C) Weatherproof bag

    D) A magnifying glass

26. Question: What should a Mail Carrier do if a package is too large for a mailbox?

    A) Leave it beside the mailbox

    B) Take it back to the post office

    C) Attempt to deliver it to the recipient's doorstep

    D) Open it to make it fit

27. Question: Which service allows recipients to receive mail at the post office rather than home?

    A) Delivery confirmation

    B) Priority Mail

    C) PO Box

    D) Express Mail

28. Question: How do Mail Carriers usually handle "Return to Sender" items?

    A) Deliver it to a neighboring address

    B) Keep it with them

    C) Deliver it back to the post office

    D) Discard it

29. Question: Which is NOT a reason mail might be undeliverable?

    A) Incomplete address

    B) Recipient moved without forwarding address

    C) The mail is postmarked

    D) The location is inaccessible

30. Question: What is the primary advantage of Priority Mail?

    A) It's always delivered within two hours

    B) It includes insurance by default

    C) It's cheaper than regular mail

    D) Faster delivery times

31. Question: What does the USPS use to ensure Mail Carriers follow their assigned routes?

A) Personal interviews

B) GPS tracking

C) Random checks

D) Feedback from recipients

32. Question: Which of the following is an essential skill for a Mail Carrier when interacting with the public?

A) Negotiation

B) Customer service

C) Coding

D) Baking

33. Question: What is typically used for safety in low visibility conditions on a Mail Carrier's vehicle?

A) Horn

B) Reflective stickers

C) Loud music

D) Fog lights

34. Question: What action should a Mail Carrier take if they suspect mail fraud?

A) Deliver the mail anyway

B) Report to their immediate supervisor

C) Confront the sender

D) Ignore it

35. Question: How often do Mail Carriers typically work?

A) Only on weekdays

B) Every day, including holidays

C) Six days a week, excluding Sundays

D) Only when there's mail to deliver

36. Question: Which service offers date-certain delivery with a money-back guarantee?

A) First-Class Mail

B) Media Mail

C) Priority Mail Express

D) Retail Ground

37. Question: Why might a Mail Carrier refuse to deliver mail to a particular address?

A) The house color is unusual

B) There's a known aggressive dog

C) The recipient is not friendly

D) It's a weekend

38. Question: Which of the following is NOT a type of mail a Mail Carrier might deliver?

A) Postcards

B) Packages

C) Emails

D) Magazines

39. Question: What should a Mail Carrier do if they accidentally damage a package?

A) Hide it

B) Report the damage and follow procedures

C) Repackage it themselves

D) Leave it at the nearest post office without informing anyone

40. Question: Which tool can help a Mail Carrier ensure timely deliveries during peak times?

A) A faster vehicle

B) Route optimization software

C) A giant mailbag

D) An alarm clock

EXAM 475 - MAIL HANDLER VEA

1. **Question:** What primary function does a Mail Handler serve in the USPS?

   A) Writing emails

   B) Delivering mail to residences

   C) Processing and sorting mail

   D) Handling customer service inquiries

2. **Question:** How do Mail Handlers ensure the safety of packages?

   A) Using protective gear only

   B) Manual inspections

   C) X-ray machines

   D) Asking customers about package contents

3. **Question:** Where do Mail Handlers primarily operate?

   A) On delivery routes

   B) At customer service counters

   C) Inside processing plants

   D) In administrative offices

4. **Question:** Which of the following is a tool Mail Handlers frequently use?

   A) Barcode scanner

   B) Delivery van

   C) Public address system

   D) Cash register

5. **Question:** In the context of a USPS facility, what does "culling" mean?

   A) Advertising mail

   B) Removing foreign items from the mail stream

   C) The final stage of sorting

   D) Digital mail scanning

6. **Question:** How do Mail Handlers contribute to efficient mail processing?

   A) By ensuring proper sorting and sequencing

   B) Through direct delivery to homes

   C) By managing postal finances

   D) Through addressing customer complaints

7. **Question:** Why is safety training crucial for Mail Handlers?

   A) To handle customer inquiries

   B) To ensure proper uniform attire

   C) To prevent workplace accidents and injuries

   D) To speed up mail delivery

8. **Question:** Which item are Mail Handlers least likely to handle?

   A) Large packages

   B) Stamped letters

   C) Customer bank details

   D) Magazines

9. **Question:** What type of mail requires special attention due to its perishable nature?

   A) Catalogs

   B) Express mail

   C) Live animals or plants

   D) Newspapers

10. **Question:** Which aspect is NOT typically a part of the Mail Handler's responsibilities?

    A) Operating mail-processing machines

    B) Transporting mail within the facility

    C) Setting postal rates

    D) Canceling stamped mail

11. **Question:** Why is it essential for Mail Handlers to stay updated on postal regulations and services?

    A) To assist customers directly

    B) To ensure mail is processed according to standards

    C) To design new stamps

    D) To decide on postal holidays

12. **Question:** Which of the following best describes the physical demands of a Mail Handler's job?

    A) Sedentary and desk-bound

    B) Mostly driving

    C) Heavy lifting and standing for extended periods

    D) Primarily typing and computer work

13. Question: In case of machinery malfunction, what should a Mail Handler do first?

    A) Attempt to repair it themselves

    B) Ignore and continue working

    C) Report to their supervisor or maintenance team

    D) Turn off all machines in the facility

14. Question: Which service ensures mail is held at the post office until the recipient picks it up?

    A) Certified Mail

    B) Priority Mail

    C) Hold Mail Service

    D) First-Class Mail

15. Question: What role do Mail Handlers play in the case of undeliverable mail?

    A) Deliver it themselves

    B) Return it to the sender directly

    C) Process it for return or disposal

    D) Store it indefinitely

16. Question: Why is teamwork crucial for Mail Handlers?

    A) To collectively decide postal policies

    B) To ensure mail is processed timely and efficiently

    C) To deliver mail to recipients

    D) To design new mail processing machines

17. Question: Which security measure helps prevent unauthorized access to USPS facilities?

    A) Open-door policy

    B) Public tours daily

    C) Badge access system

    D) Allowing all vehicles inside

18. Question: How do Mail Handlers ensure the right mail gets loaded onto the correct transportation method?

    A) Guessing based on package size

    B) Relying on memory

    C) Using system-generated labels and barcodes

    D) Asking customers directly

19. Question: Why is continuous training essential for Mail Handlers?

    A) To shift to delivery roles

    B) To keep updated with new machinery and regulations

    C) To take over administrative tasks

    D) To engage with customers directly

20. Question: In what scenario might a Mail Handler interact directly with a customer?

    A) Delivering mail to their home

    B) When a customer visits a processing facility for a package

    C) Setting postal rates

    D) Designing new stamps

21. Question: Which of these is a critical safety precaution Mail Handlers should take?

    A) Wearing headphones while working

    B) Using machinery without gloves

    C) Carrying packages using proper lifting techniques

    D) Racing against the clock to speed up processing

22. Question: What's Mail Handlers' primary challenge during the holiday season?

    A) Reduced mail volume

    B) Longer break times

    C) Increased mail volume

    D) Fewer working hours

23. Question: What role does automation play in the mail-handling process?

    A) Decreases efficiency

    B) Makes manual sorting more prevalent

    C) Streamlines and speeds up sorting

    D) Makes the mail handling job redundant

24. Question: Which item will most likely be sorted using a Flat Sorting Machine?

    A) A postcard

    B) A small parcel

    C) A standard letter

    D) A thick catalog

25. Question: For a Mail Handler, what is the primary goal of sequencing?

A) Assigning prices to mail

B) Organizing mail according to delivery routes

C) Checking mail content

D) Designing postal stamps

26. Question: How do Mail Handlers contribute to the USPS sustainability efforts?

A) By planting trees

B) Ensuring proper disposal or recycling of undeliverable mail

C) By reducing mail prices

D) Interacting with customers directly

27. Question: What does a Mail Handler primarily use a conveyor belt for?

A) For personal transportation

B) To charge electronic devices

C) To transport sorted mail to designated areas

D) To interact with customers

28. Question: Why is time management crucial for Mail Handlers?

A) To enjoy longer breaks

B) To ensure timely processing and dispatch of mail

C) To set postal rates

D) To design mail-handling machines

29. Question: How do Mail Handlers ensure fragile items are treated with care?

A) They shake each package

B) They use "Fragile" labels and place them in designated areas

C) They store them with heavy items

D) They leave them unattended

30. Question: How do Mail Handlers assist during natural disasters or emergencies?

A) By halting all mail processes

B) By ensuring critical mail like medicines or emergency communications are prioritized

C) By personally delivering all mail

D) By taking over administrative roles

31. Question: What purpose does the Optical Character Reader (OCR) serve in mail handling?

    A) Scanning and reading handwritten addresses

    B) Weighing parcels

    C) Taking photographs of mail items

    D) Painting over graffiti on mailboxes

32. Question: What would immediate action be if a suspicious package is identified?

    A) Open it to inspect the contents

    B) Alert the appropriate authorities and follow established protocols

    C) Move it to another conveyor belt

    D) Place it in the general delivery area

33. Question: Which type of mail requires a secure chain of custody?

    A) Regular flyers

    B) Magazines

    C) Registered Mail

    D) Postcards

34. Question: How are Mail Handlers involved in "revenue protection" for the USPS?

    A) They set postal rates

    B) They sell postal products

    C) They ensure proper postage is applied to mail

    D) They invest in stock markets

35. Question: Why is teamwork essential among Mail Handlers?

    A) To get promoted quickly

    B) To ensure efficient and seamless mail processing

    C) To reduce individual responsibilities

    D) To have longer break times

36. Question: What is a critical focus in training for new Mail Handlers?

    A) Customer service skills

    B) Equipment and safety protocols

    C) Corporate history of the USPS

    D) Stamp collecting

37. Question: What is a critical quality that Mail Handlers must possess?

   A) Multilingualism

   B) Ability to lift heavy items

   C) Artistic skills

   D) Acting skills

38. Question: Why is continual learning important for Mail Handlers?

   A) To become a Mail Carrier

   B) To keep abreast of new postal technologies and methods

   C) To diversify into different roles

   D) To take more holidays

39. Question: What would Mail Handlers do with undeliverable mail with no return address?

   A) Discard it immediately

   B) Send it to the Mail Recovery Center

   C) Open it to find clues

   D) Leave it on their desk indefinitely

40. Question: What tool is primarily used for moving large sacks of mail?

   A) A ladder

   B) A sack barrow

   C) A forklift

   D) A hand fan

EXAM 477 - CUSTOMER SERVICE/CLERK VEA

1. **Question:** What is the primary responsibility of a postal service clerk?

   A) Driving the delivery van

   B) Sorting mail at the central facility

   C) Assisting customers at the service counter

   D) Designing new stamps

2. **Question:** Why is knowledge about USPS products and services essential for a postal clerk?

   A) It's necessary for promotion

   B) To recommend and guide customers effectively

   C) Only to pass the VEA exam

   D) It's not essential

3. **Question:** How do clerks handle customer complaints?

   A) By continually refunding money

   B) Ignoring them until they go away

   C) Using standardized protocols and ensuring customer satisfaction

   D) Directing them to another postal service

4. **Question:** Which technology is frequently used by clerks for package tracking?

   A) A barcode scanner

   B) A radio signal transmitter

   C) A magnifying glass

   D) A voice recorder

5. **Question:** What should clerks do if unsure about a specific postal regulation or service?

   A) Guess the answer

   B) Ask the customer for advice

   C) Refer to official USPS resources or ask a supervisor

   D) Avoid the question

6. **Question:** Why are interpersonal skills critical for a postal clerk?

   A) To handle packages better

   B) To negotiate postal rates

   C) To engage effectively with customers and colleagues

   D) To design the layout of the post office

7. **Question:** How do clerks ensure the correct postage is applied to a package?

   A) By shaking the package

   B) Weighing it and referring to postage rate charts

   C) Guessing the weight

   D) Asking the sender its value

8. **Question:** Why is it vital for postal clerks to remain updated on postal regulations and price changes?

   A) To pass the time during slow days

   B) To engage in debates with customers

   C) To ensure compliance and provide accurate information to customers

   D) Only for annual reviews

9. **Question:** Which of the following is a specialized service that USPS offers for secure mailing?

   A) Priority Mail Express

   B) Media Mail

   C) First-Class Mail

   D) Registered Mail

10. **Question:** Why might a clerk suggest Priority Mail Express to a customer?

    A) For bulk mailing

    B) When overnight delivery is required

    C) If the customer is mailing a postcard

    D) When sending fragile items, only

11. **Question:** What action do clerks typically take for mail without an undeliverable return address?

    A) Store it indefinitely

    B) Open it to find a clue

    C) Send it to the Dead Letter Office or Mail Recovery Center

    D) Immediately discard it

12. **Question:** Which USPS service offers date-certain delivery with a money-back guarantee?

    A) Media Mail

    B) Priority Mail Express

    C) Standard Post

    D) First-Class Mail

13. **Question:** Why is the "Hold for Pickup" service beneficial?

   A) It allows for faster delivery.

   B) It ensures the recipient gets their mail directly at the post office.

   C) It reduces postage costs.

   D) It includes insurance automatically.

14. **Question:** In which scenario is the "Return Receipt" service most valuable?

   A) When mailing a birthday card

   B) Sending a standard letter to a friend

   C) Mailing legal documents that require proof of delivery

   D) Sending a postcard while on vacation

15. **Question:** What does the ZIP in "ZIP Code" stand for?

   A) Zonal Improvement Plan

   B) Zonal Identification Protocol

   C) Zone Improvement Protocol

   D) Zone Improvement Plan

16. **Question:** What additional service might a clerk suggest for customers wanting to mail items internationally for added peace of mind?

   A) Priority Mail International with tracking

   B) Domestic First-Class Mail

   C) Media Mail

   D) Local pickup service

17. **Question:** How can clerks assist customers in determining the best shipping option for their needs?

   A) By guessing the customer's preferences

   B) Solely by recommending the most expensive option

   C) Through a thorough understanding of USPS services and asking the customer specific questions

   D) By avoiding the question entirely

18. **Question:** What is the typical suggestion if a customer's package exceeds the weight limit for First-Class Mail?

   A) Priority Mail

   B) Standard Post

   C) Return it to the customer

   D) Use two First-Class stamps

19. Question: Why might a postal clerk suggest using a Flat Rate Box to a customer?

   A) Because it's the cheapest option for all mail

   B) For items that are heavy but fit inside the box, as the price is the same regardless of weight

   C) Only for international shipments

   D) To promote a new USPS initiative

20. Question: Which of the following does the USPS offer specifically for businesses?

   A) Business Reply Mail

   B) Birthday Greeting Service

   C) Package Party Delivery

   D) Mail-Forwarding-Only Service

21. Question: A customer approaches the counter with a fragile item. What's the clerk's best suggestion to ensure it remains intact during transit?

   A) Wrap it in a cloth

   B) Use Priority Mail Express for faster delivery

   C) Use cushioned mailers or bubble wrap, and mark the package as "Fragile."

   D) Use a "Fragile" sticker without any additional packaging

22. Question: How might a clerk handle a customer unsure about the address they're sending mail?

   A) Ask them to guess the address

   B) Refuse the mail item

   C) Suggest they verify the address before mailing

   D) Send the mail to the closest approximation of the address

23. Question: What additional service might a clerk recommend for a customer sending a valuable item?

   A) A greeting card service

   B) An overnight delivery, regardless of urgency

   C) Insurance and tracking for the mail piece

   D) A discount coupon for their next visit

24. Question: A customer sends a document and wants confirmation once the recipient signs it. What service should the clerk suggest?

   A) Standard First-Class Mail

   B) Media Mail with tracking

   C) Priority Mail with return receipt

   D) Priority Mail Express with a greeting card

25. Question: What is the significance of the Intelligent Mail Barcode (IM**B**) seen on some mail pieces?

A) It's purely decorative.

B) It's a QR code for special offers.

C) It provides tracking information and assists in mail processing.

D) It indicates that the mail is international.

26. Question: If a customer wants to send a book, which is the most cost-effective service a clerk might suggest?

A) Priority Mail Express

B) First-Class Mail

C) Media Mail

D) Business Reply Mail

27. Question: What should a clerk do if a customer's mail piece exceeds the maximum dimensions for First-Class Mail?

A) Fold the item to make it fit

B) Recommend another suitable USPS service

C) Suggest using two stamps

D) Refuse to mail the item

28. Question: How can clerks ensure a smooth experience during busy periods at the post office?

A) By taking breaks frequently

B) By assisting one customer thoroughly before moving to the next

C) By rushing through transactions

D) By multitasking and not focusing on any single task

29. Question: Which service should a clerk recommend for time-sensitive mail that needs to be delivered the next day?

A) Media Mail

B) Priority Mail

C) First-Class Mail

D) Priority Mail Express

30. Question: A customer needs clarification about the postage required for their mail. How can the clerk assist?

A) Estimate the postage and hope for the best

B) Use a postal scale to determine the exact postage

C) Suggest using multiple stamps to ensure it's enough

D) Advise the customer to seek guidance elsewhere

31. Question: Why is it essential for a clerk to stay updated on USPS policies and services?

   A) To impress their coworkers

   B) To ensure accurate guidance and efficient service to customers

   C) To participate in annual USPS quizzes

   D) To earn extra vacation days

ANSWER KEY

After rigorously testing one's knowledge through questions and practice tests, the Answer Key section emerges as a crucial tool for self-assessment. It provides detailed solutions and explanations for each query, ensuring that candidates know the correct answers and understand the rationale behind them. This section is a testament to our commitment to comprehensive learning, where understanding the 'why' is as vital as knowing the 'what'.

EXAM 955 - MAINTENANCE AND ELECTRONICS

1. **Answer: C)** Voltage

   Reason: Voltage is the electric potential that pushes electrons to move in a circuit, leading to electric current. While the other components mentioned can influence or be influenced by the movement of electrons, the voltage drives them.

2. **Answer: D)** Ohm's Law

   Reason: Ohm's Law states that the current (I) through a conductor between two points is directly proportional to the voltage (V) across the two points when the temperature remains constant.

3. **Answer: B)** Reverse Bias

   Reason: A diode is forward-biased when the P-side (anode) is connected to the positive terminal, and the N-side (cathode) is connected to the negative terminal. This configuration is opposite in reverse Bias, and the diode does not conduct.

4. **Answer: D)** Capacitor

   Reason: Capacitors store energy in an electric field between their plates. When voltage is applied across a capacitor, an electric field develops, storing energy that can be released later.

5. **Answer: B)** Generator

   Reason: A generator typically converts mechanical energy from an engine or turbine into electrical energy. Motors, on the other hand, do the opposite, converting electrical energy to automatic.

6. **Answer: C)** A current-controlled current source

   Reason: A transistor primarily acts as a current-controlled current source. While it can perform switching operations and amplify signals, its fundamental behavior is to control current flow based on an input current.

7. **Answer: B)** Increase or decrease voltage levels

   Reason: Transformers work on the principle of electromagnetic induction and are used to increase (step-up) or decrease (step-down) voltage levels without changing the frequency.

8. **Answer: D)** Capacitor

   Reason: Circuits often use capacitors to filter or remove specific frequency components. Depending on their configuration, they can act as high-pass or low-pass filters.

9. **Answer: B)** Same through all components

   Reason: In a series circuit, all components are connected end-to-end, meaning the same current flows through every element.

10. **Answer: D)** Its resistance value

Reason: The color bands on a resistor serve as a code to determine its resistance value. The bars are decoded using a standard color chart.

11. **Answer: C)** Capacitor

Reason: Capacitors allow AC signals to pass through them but block DC. This property is helpful in coupling and decoupling applications in circuits.

12. **Answer: A)** Increases

Reason: In semiconductors, as temperature increases, more electrons are excited into the conduction band, leading to increased conductivity.

13. **Answer: B)** Convert AC to DC

Reason: A rectifier's primary function is to convert alternating current (A**C)** to direct current (DC). It does this by allowing current to flow in only one direction.

14. **Answer: B)** Parallel

Reason: Components are connected across common points or junctions in parallel circuits. This means they share the same voltage but may carry different currents.

15. **Answer: D)** Transistor

Reason: Transistors, particularly Bipolar Junction Transistors (BJTs) and Field-Effect Transistors (FETs), are widely used as amplifying devices in electronic circuits due to their ability to amplify electrical signals.

16. **Answer: C)** Farad

Reason: The unit of capacitance is the Farad, symbolized as "F." It represents the amount of electric charge stored for a given electric potential.

17. **Answer: D)** NOR

Reason: The NOR gate, a combination of an OR gate followed by a NOT gate, only provides an output of "1" when all its inputs are low or "0".

18. **Answer: C)** Ohm's Law

Reason: Ohm's Law, named after the German physicist Georg Simon Ohm, states that the current (I) through a conductor is directly proportional to the voltage (V) across it and inversely proportional to its resistance (R). It's given by the formula I = V/R.

19. **Answer: C)** Allow current flow in one direction

Reason: A diode is a semiconductor device that allows current to flow in only one direction, offering high resistance in the other direction. This unidirectional behavior is fundamental in rectification processes.

20. **Answer: C)** Electrolytic

Reason: Electrolytic capacitors are polarized, meaning they have a positive and negative terminal. They must be connected with the correct circuit polarity; otherwise, they might get damaged or explode.

21. **Answer: C)** Spike

Reason: A spike refers to a sudden and sharp rise in voltage, lasting for a concise duration. It's a type of electrical disturbance that can damage electronic devices.

22. **Answer: C)** NAND

Reason: The NAND gate provides an output inverse inverse of the AND gate. Thus, a NAND gate produces a low output only when both inputs are high.

EXAM STUDY GUIDE

23. Answer: C) Variable capacitor

Reason: Variable capacitors, also known as tuning capacitors, are used to tune radio frequencies in applications like AM radio receivers. By adjusting the capacitance, different stations can be tuned in.

24. Answer: C) Inductance

Reason: Inductance is a property of an electrical circuit by which a change in current induces an electromotive force (EMF). It opposes the difference in the recent course. This is especially prevalent in coils and inductors.

25. Answer: B) Core

Reason: The core of a transformer, usually made of iron or ferrite, provides a path for the magnetic flux, aiding in the transfer of energy from the primary to the secondary winding.

26. Answer: B) Motor

Reason: A motor converts electrical energy into mechanical energy, causing motion. Engines can be found in various household and industrial applications.

27. Answer: C) Frequency Modulation (FM)

Reason: In Frequency Modulation (FM), the frequency of the carrier wave varies following the amplitude of the input signal. This type of modulation is commonly used in FM radio broadcasting.

28. Answer: C) Convert AC to DC

Reason: A rectifier's primary function is to convert alternating current (A**C**) to direct current (DC). It's essential for powering electronic devices that require DC power from an AC source.

29. Answer: A) Two p-type materials separated by an n-type

Reason: A PNP transistor consists of two p-type materials separated by an n-type material. This arrangement allows for the flow of holes (positive charge carriers) as the primary current.

30. Answer: B) Varistor

Reason: A varistor functions as a two-terminal, non-linear resistor. Its resistance varies with voltage. Varistors are often used to protect circuits from excessive voltage.

31. Answer: A) It measures the quality of resonance in a circuit.

Reason: The Q-factor, or Quality factor, measures the resonance quality in a circuit. A higher Q-factor indicates a lower rate of energy loss and a sharper resonance.

32. Answer: D) Capacitor

Reason: A capacitor is used to store electric charge temporarily. It consists of two conductive plates separated by an insulating material, and its ability to store energy is measured in Farads.

33. Answer: D) XOR

Reason: The XOR (Exclusive OR) gate produces a high output only when its two inputs differ. If both inputs are the same, its production is low.

34. Answer: B) Tunnel Diode

Reason: The tunnel diode utilizes the quantum tunneling effect to operate. This gives it a negative resistance region in its voltage-current characteristic curve, making it useful for specific high-frequency applications.

35. Answer: C) Dissipate heat

Reason: A heat sink is designed to efficiently dissipate heat away from a hot component, such as a processor or a power transistor, to prevent overheating and ensure the smooth operation of the element.

36. Answer: C) Ohm's Law

Reason: Ohm's Law defines the relationship between voltage, current, and resistance in an electrical circuit. It states that the voltage across a conductor is proportional to the recent passing when the temperature remains constant.

37. Answer: B) Power

Reason: Power in an electrical system refers to the rate at which work is done or energy is transferred. It is calculated by multiplying the voltage by the current in the circuit.

38. Answer: B) Amplifier

Reason: An amplifier's primary function is to increase the strength or amplitude of an input signal. This can be used in various applications, from audio and communication devices.

39. Answer: D) Quartz Crystal

Reason: The piezoelectric effect is prominent in quartz crystals, where mechanical deformation leads to voltage generation and vice versa. This effect is used in devices like crystal oscillators in clocks and radios.

40. Answer: C) Light Emitting Diode (LED)

Reason: LEDs, or light-emitting diodes, are semiconductors emitting light when an electric current flows through them. They use a p-n junction to produce light efficiently, commonly found in display screens, indicators, and general lighting.

41. Answer: D) Switch circuits

Reason: A relay is an electrically operated switch. It provides isolation between control and controlled circuits, allowing low-power signals to control high-power circuits.

42. Answer: D) QED

Reason: QED, or Quantum Electrodynamics, is a theory in physics and not a type of transistor. BJT, FET, and MOSFET are different electronic circuit transistors.

43. Answer: B) Two

Reason: A bistable multivibrator, a flip-flop, has two stable states. This makes it essential for memory elements and binary systems, as it can represent the two binary digits, 0 and 1.

EXAM 474 - MAIL CARRIER VEA

1. **Answer: B)** Delivering mail to recipients

    Reason: A Mail Carrier's primary responsibility is to ensure timely and accurate delivery of mail, parcels, and other post to recipients along their designated routes.

2. **Answer: B)** Daily

    Reason: Mail Carriers typically deliver mail daily, except on Sundays and federal holidays.

3. **Answer: B)** Mail satchel

    Reason: Mail Carriers use mail satchels to carry and organize mail during their delivery routes.

4. **Answer: B)** Snow

    Reason: Snow can impede mail delivery by blocking roads and making conditions hazardous for Mail Carriers.

5. **Answer: A)** Avoiding animals like dogs

    Reason: Mail Carriers should be cautious of animals, especially dogs, to avoid potential attacks or disruptions during mail delivery.

6. **Answer: B)** Return it to the post office

    Reason: Mail Carriers are trained to return mail to the post office for further processing or holding if it needs to be delivered.

7. **Answer: C)** Increased mail volume

    Reason: The holiday season often sees a surge in mail volume due to gift sending, cards, and online shopping, making it a busy period for Mail Carriers.

8. **Answer: C)** LLVs (Long Life Vehicles)

    Reason: LLVs are explicitly designed for mail delivery and are commonly used by Mail Carriers, especially in suburban areas.

9. **Answer: D)** Certified mail

    Reason: Certified mail provides the sender with a mailing receipt and requires the recipient's signature upon delivery for verification.

10. **Answer: A)** GPS devices

    Reason: GPS devices help Mail Carriers navigate their routes more efficiently, ensuring timely delivery.

11. **Answer: D)** USPS

    Reason: The United States Postal Service (USPS) is the federal agency responsible for providing mail delivery service and setting the guidelines, standards, and regulations for mail delivery throughout the country.

12. **Answer: B)** If the recipient is on vacation

    Reason: If a recipient is on vacation or temporarily away, they can request the USPS to hold their mail, ensuring it's secured. This service helps protect mail from theft or weather damage.

13. **Answer: B)** Deliver them with extra care

    Reason: Fragile items can break or get damaged easily during transport. Mail Carriers need to handle these items with utmost care to ensure they reach the recipient in good condition. This often involves being gentle when placing them into the delivery vehicle, ensuring they don't get squashed by heavier items, and delivering them to avoid jostling or dropping.

14. **Answer: C)** Knowledge of local delivery routes

   Reason: Familiarity with local delivery routes allows Mail Carriers to be efficient in their deliveries, navigate any obstacles or detours, and ensure timely and accurate delivery of mail and packages to the recipients.

15. **Answer: B)** A comfortable pair of shoes

   Reason: Mail Carriers, especially those on walking routes, spend a significant portion of their day on their feet. A comfortable pair of shoes is vital to support them throughout the day, prevent foot fatigue, and reduce the risk of injuries.

16. **Answer: A)** The Mail Carrier leaves a notice

   Reason: The Mail Carrier will leave a notice if a package requires a signature or cannot be left safely and the recipient isn't home. This notice informs the recipient about the delivery attempt and provides instructions on retrieving the package or scheduling a redelivery.

17. **Answer: B)** By using protective coverings and gear

   Reason: To protect mail and packages from the elements, especially rain, Mail Carriers use protective coverings like plastic sheaths and wear gear like raincoats and hats. This ensures that the contents remain dry and undamaged during delivery.

18. **Answer: D)** Busy intersections

   Reason: Busy intersections pose potential dangers for Mail Carriers due to high traffic volume and the risk of accidents. Carriers must be cautious and vigilant when navigating these areas to ensure their safety and the safety of others.

19. **Answer: B)** Priority Mail Express

   Reason: Priority Mail Express is the USPS's fastest mail service, offering guaranteed delivery, tracking, and notifications to the sender and recipient. This ensures that both parties know the package's status and expected delivery time.

20. **Answer: B)** To ensure timely delivery

   Reason: A Mail Carrier's knowledge of their assigned routes enables them to navigate the area efficiently, promptly address any challenges, and make timely deliveries. This familiarity aids in avoiding delays, ensuring recipients get their mail and packages as expected.

21. **Answer: C)** Ensuring timely delivery of mail and packages

   Reason: While Mail Carriers may participate in various tasks, their primary duty is ensuring that mail and packages reach their intended recipients on time.

22. **Answer: B)** Knowledge of postal regulations

   Reason: While knowledge of postal regulations is crucial for the job, it isn't a physical requirement. The other options list physical capacities essential for daily tasks.

23. **Answer: D)** Avoid eye contact and back away slowly

   Reason: Avoiding direct eye contact and backing away slowly is the recommended approach when faced with an aggressive dog to prevent triggering an attack.

24. **Answer: C)** Sorting and organizing mail for delivery

   Reason: Before beginning their routes, Mail Carriers typically start by sorting and organizing the mail and packages for efficient delivery.

25. **Answer: C)** Weatherproof bag

   Reason: A weatherproof bag can protect mail and packages from elements like rain or snow, ensuring they remain undamaged.

26. Answer: C) Attempt to deliver it to the recipient's doorstep

> **Reason:** If the package is too large for the mailbox, the correct procedure is to try and give it directly to the recipient's doorstep, ensuring it's safely placed.

27. Answer: C) PO Box

> **Reason:** A PO Box (Post Office Box) is a service where recipients can rent a box within the post office to receive mail rather than getting deliveries at home.

28. Answer: C) Deliver it back to the post office

> **Reason:** "Return to Sender" items are typically taken back to the post office for processing and eventually returned to the original sender.

29. Answer: C) The mail is postmarked

> **Reason:** Postmarking is a standard process for all mail and does not make it undeliverable. The other options can prevent successful delivery.

30. Answer: D) Faster delivery times

> **Reason:** Priority Mail is designed to offer expedited delivery compared to regular mail, ensuring that the items reach their destinations quicker.

31. Answer: B) GPS tracking

> **Reason:** GPS tracking helps USPS monitor and ensure that Mail Carriers adhere to their assigned routes and make timely deliveries.

32. Answer: B) Customer service

> **Reason:** Mail Carriers often interact with the public during their deliveries, making customer service skills vital for positive interactions and addressing concerns.

33. Answer: B) Reflective stickers

> **Reason:** Reflective stickers increase the vehicle's visibility in low light conditions, helping to prevent accidents.

34. Answer: B) Report to their immediate supervisor

> **Reason:** If a Mail Carrier suspects mail fraud, the correct protocol is to report it to their supervisor to ensure it's adequately investigated.

35. Answer: C) Six days a week, excluding Sundays

> **Reason:** Typically, Mail Carriers work six days a week, with Sundays being the standard of the day, although there are exceptions for some package deliveries.

36. Answer: C) Priority Mail Express

> **Reason:** Priority Mail Express ensures the fastest, date-certain service with a money-back guarantee, offering peace of mind to the sender.

37. Answer: B) There's a known aggressive dog

> **Reason:** Mail Carriers may refuse delivery if an aggressive dog threatens their safety. Safety concerns always take precedence.

38. Answer: C) Emails

> **Reason:** Emails are digital and not delivered by Mail Carriers. The other options are all tangible items that Mail Carriers deliver.

39. Answer: B) Report the damage and follow procedures

> **Reason:** If a package is damaged, the Mail Carrier must report it and follow the established USPS procedures to address the situation.

40. Answer: B) Route optimization software

Reason: Route optimization software can provide the most efficient paths, ensuring timely deliveries, especially during peak mail and package delivery times.

EXAM 475 - MAIL HANDLER VEA

1. **Answer: C)** Processing and sorting mail

   Reason: While the USPS has various roles, Mail Handlers specifically deal with the internal task of processing and sorting mail, ensuring it's ready for the next stage of delivery or distribution.

2. **Answer: C)** X-ray machines

   Reason: To enhance security and safety, Mail Handlers use X-ray machines to screen packages, especially in extensive facilities, ensuring they don't contain hazardous or prohibited items.

3. **Answer: C)** Inside processing plants

   Reason: Mail Handlers mainly work in USPS processing plants where mail is sorted and prepared for distribution, playing a pivotal role in the mail transit process.

4. **Answer: A)** Barcode scanner

   Reason: Mail Handlers often use barcode scanners to read the information on parcels and letters, helping in the efficient and automated sorting process within USPS facilities.

5. **Answer: B)** Removing foreign items from the mail stream

   Reason: Culling is the process of manually or mechanically sifting through mail to remove items that are too large or thick, or that might cause jams or issues in the sorting machines.

6. **Answer: A)** By ensuring proper sorting and sequencing

   Reason: Mail Handlers play a crucial role in the internal workings of the USPS. By accurately sorting and sequencing mail, they ensure that deliveries are timely and go to the correct addresses, thus maintaining the efficiency and reliability of the postal service.

7. **Answer: C)** To prevent workplace accidents and injuries

   Reason: Given the nature of their job, which involves handling machinery, heavy parcels, and continuous movement, safety training is paramount for Mail Handlers. This training ensures they operate in a manner that minimizes risks to themselves and their colleagues.

8. **Answer: C)** Customer bank details

   Reason: Mail Handlers deal with physical mail items. They don't handle sensitive personal or financial information like customer bank details, which is more related to administrative or digital tasks.

9. **Answer: C)** Live animals or plants

   Reason: Live animals or plants are perishable items that might be time-sensitive or require special handling conditions. Mail Handlers must be aware of these items to ensure they're processed quickly and carefully.

10. **Answer: C)** Setting postal rates

    Reason: Setting postal rates involves decision-making at higher administrative or regulatory levels. Mail Handlers focus on operational tasks within the facility, ensuring smooth processing and movement of mail.

11. Answer: B) To ensure mail is processed according to standards

Reason: By staying updated on regulations and services, Mail Handlers can ensure they process items correctly, adhering to the standards and rules set by USPS. This knowledge helps maintain service quality and compliance.

12. Answer: C) Heavy lifting and standing for extended periods

Reason: Mail Handlers often deal with bulky packages and continuously move, sort, and process mail, requiring them to be on their feet for extended durations and frequently lift heavy items.

13. Answer: C) Report to their supervisor or maintenance team

Reason: Safety and proper operation are paramount. If a machine malfunctions, a Mail Handler should report it to ensure experts address the issue and prevent potential hazards or further damage.

14. Answer: C) Hold Mail Service

Reason: The Hold Mail Service is designed to retain mail safely at the post office until the recipient can retrieve it, ensuring its security during the individual's absence.

15. Answer: C) Process it for return or disposal

Reason: When mail is undeliverable, Mail Handlers help process it, ensuring it either gets returned to the sender or is properly disposed of if it cannot be returned.

16. Answer: B) To ensure mail is processed timely and efficiently

Reason: Within a USPS processing plant, Mail Handlers often work alongside other personnel. Collaborative teamwork ensures the efficient mail flow through the system, from receiving to dispatching.

17. Answer: C) Badge access system

Reason: To maintain the mail's security and integrity and personnel's safety, facilities often employ badge access systems. These ensure that only authorized personnel can access specific areas.

18. Answer: C) Using system-generated labels and barcodes

Reason: System-generated labels and barcodes provide accurate information about each mail item's destination and transportation method. Mail Handlers rely on this to ensure proper dispatch.

19. Answer: B) To keep updated with new machinery and regulations

Reason: The postal environment evolves with the introduction of new machinery, technologies, and regulations. Continuous training ensures Mail Handlers can operate effectively in this changing landscape.

20. Answer: B) When a customer visits a processing facility for a package

Reason: While Mail Handlers primarily work behind the scenes, there might be instances where customers visit a processing facility for reasons like package retrieval, and a Mail Handler might interact with them in such scenarios.

21. Answer: C) Carrying packages using proper lifting techniques

Reason: Proper lifting techniques are essential to prevent injuries. By using these techniques, Mail Handlers can handle heavy items safely and reduce the risk of strain or injury.

22. Answer: C) Increased mail volume

Reason: During the holiday season, the mail volume typically spikes. Mail Handlers have to manage and process a more significant number of packages and letters in these peak times, ensuring timely deliveries.

23. **Answer: C)** Streamlines and speeds up sorting

   Reason: Automation allows for quicker and more accurate sorting through advanced machines and technologies. While Mail Handlers are essential, automation aids them in processing vast amounts of mail efficiently.

24. **Answer: D)** A thick catalog

   Reason: Flat Sorting Machines (FSM) are designed to handle "flats," larger than regular letters but not as bulky as parcels. Items like magazines or thick catalogs would be processed using FSMs.

25. **Answer: B)** Organizing mail according to delivery routes

   Reason: Sequencing helps organize the mail to align with the delivery routes. This arrangement assists carriers in delivering mail in a streamlined manner without needing to sort it themselves.

26. **Answer: B)** Ensuring proper disposal or recycling of undeliverable mail

   Reason: Part of the USPS's sustainability efforts involves the responsible disposal or recycling of undeliverable mail. Mail Handlers play a role in ensuring such correspondence is correctly processed to minimize environmental impact.

27. **Answer: C)** To transport sorted mail to designated areas

   Reason: Conveyor belts in USPS processing facilities help move mail efficiently from one processing stage to the next or designated areas for further handling or dispatch.

28. **Answer: B)** To ensure timely processing and dispatch of mail

   Reason: Mail Handlers deal with vast volumes of mail. Efficient time management ensures that mail is sorted, processed, and dispatched within the required timeframes, maintaining the reputation of timely delivery that the USPS upholds.

29. **Answer: B)** They use "Fragile" labels and place them in designated areas

   Reason: "Fragile" labels indicate that the contents of a package are delicate and need special attention. Mail Handlers ensure these packages are placed in designated areas and are handled with extra care to prevent damage.

30. **Answer: B)** By ensuring critical mail like medicines or emergency communications are prioritized

   Reason: During emergencies, certain mail items become even more critical. Mail Handlers prioritize essential items, ensuring they are processed and delivered promptly, even amidst challenging situations.

31. **Answer: A)** Scanning and reading handwritten addresses

   Reason: The Optical Character Reader (OCR) is a technological tool used in mail processing centers to scan and recognize handwritten or typed addresses. This automation speeds up the sorting process, enhancing operational efficiency.

32. **Answer: B)** Alert the appropriate authorities and follow established protocols

   Reason: If a suspicious package is identified, the proper procedure is to alert the relevant authorities immediately. This is crucial for ensuring the safety of both the workers and the public.

33. **Answer: C)** Registered Mail

   Reason: Registered Mail is a specialized service that offers enhanced security measures. It involves a secure chain of custody to ensure the mail's safety and accountability from the sender to the receiver.

34. **Answer: C)** They ensure proper postage is applied to mail

   Reason: Mail Handlers are involved in "revenue protection" by providing all mail items with the appropriate postage. This is a crucial step in preventing revenue leakage for the USPS.

35. Answer: B) To ensure efficient and seamless mail processing

Reason: Teamwork allows Mail Handlers to coordinate effectively, especially during high-volume or peak periods. This ensures that the workflow is optimized for efficient and accurate mail processing.

36. Answer: B) Equipment and safety protocols

Reason: Training for new Mail Handlers primarily focuses on familiarizing them with the equipment they will be using and the safety protocols they must follow. This prepares them for the rigorous and demanding tasks they will handle.

37. Answer: B) Ability to lift heavy items

Reason: Given that Mail Handlers deal with varying sizes and weights of parcels and mail, the ability to lift heavy items safely is a critical skill they must possess.

38. Answer: B) To keep abreast of new postal technologies and methods

Reason: Postal services are constantly evolving with new technologies and methods. Mail Handlers must continually learn to adapt to these changes and maintain efficiency.

39. Answer: B) Send it to the Mail Recovery Center

Reason: Undeliverable mail with no return address is sent to the Mail Recovery Center, where efforts are made to return it to the sender or recipient, or it may be auctioned, donated, or properly disposed of.

40. Answer: C) A forklift

Reason: Forklifts are mainly used for lifting and moving large, heavy sacks of mail or palletized goods in the mail processing facility. They are essential tools for managing significant volumes of mail.

EXAM 477 - CUSTOMER SERVICE/CLERK VEA

1. Answer: C) Assisting customers at the service counter

Reason: Postal service clerks primarily interface with customers directly at the service counter, offering services such as mailing packages, selling stamps, and answering postal-related queries.

2. Answer: B) To recommend and guide customers effectively

Reason: A comprehensive understanding of USPS products and services equips clerks to assist and guide customers more efficiently, ensuring they choose the best services for their needs, leading to optimal customer satisfaction.

3. Answer: C) Using standardized protocols and ensuring customer satisfaction

Reason: Handling customer complaints requires adherence to established protocols, ensuring customers feel valued and their concerns are addressed. This resolves the immediate issue and helps maintain trust in the USPS.

4. Answer: A) A barcode scanner

Reason: Barcode scanners scan tracking numbers on packages, accessing information regarding the package's current status, previous locations, and estimated delivery. This technology is central to modern mail tracking and customer assurance.

5. **Answer: C)** Refer to official USPS resources or ask a supervisor

   Reason: Clerks must provide accurate and reliable information. If they need clarification, consulting official USPS resources or seeking guidance from a supervisor ensures that customers receive correct information.

6. **Answer: C)** To engage effectively with customers and colleagues

   Reason: Interpersonal skills allow clerks to communicate effectively, handle disputes, and build customer rapport. Good interpersonal relations also facilitate smooth operations within the postal office team.

7. **Answer: B)** Weighing it and referring to postage rate charts

   Reason: The correct postage is determined by weighing packages and cross-referencing their weight with the current postal rates. This method ensures accuracy and fairness in charges.

8. **Answer: C)** To ensure compliance and provide accurate information to customers

   Reason: Keeping updated ensures that clerks adhere to regulations and avoid potential customer disputes. Providing accurate pricing and regulatory information maintains the USPS's reputation for reliability and transparency.

9. **Answer: D)** Registered Mail

   Reason: Registered Mail provides the highest level of mail security, ensuring a chain of custody and offering options like insurance. It's often chosen for sending valuable or essential items.

10. **Answer: B)** When overnight delivery is required

    Reason: Priority Mail Express is the USPS's fastest delivery service, offering guaranteed overnight delivery. Clerks might suggest this service to customers with time-sensitive mail needs.

11. **Answer: C)** Send it to the Dead Letter Office or Mail Recovery Center

    Reason: The Dead Letter Office, now often called the Mail Recovery Center, handles undeliverable mail and lacks a return address. They attempt to find its rightful recipient or sender. If this proves impossible, the mail might be auctioned, donated, or disposed of, depending on its nature.

12. **Answer: B)** Priority Mail Express

    Reason: Priority Mail Express is the United States Postal Service's quickest mail service, ensuring overnight or next-day delivery. If they fail to meet the delivery time, customers receive a money-back guarantee.

13. **Answer: B)** It ensures the recipient gets their mail directly at the post office.

    Reason: The "Hold for Pickup" service ensures that mail or packages are held at the local post office, allowing recipients to pick them up personally. This can be especially useful for essential items or those who might not be home to receive them.

14. **Answer: C)** Mailing legal documents that require proof of delivery

    Reason: The "Return Receipt" service provides proof of delivery, making it invaluable for sending essential documents like legal or contractual papers where the sender requires evidence that the recipient received the item.

15. **Answer: D)** Zone Improvement Plan

    Reason: ZIP stands for "Zone Improvement Plan." Introduced in 1963, the ZIP Code system was developed to streamline and improve mail delivery efficiency across the United States.

16. **Answer: A)** Priority Mail International with tracking

    Reason: Priority Mail International offers reliable international mail services and includes tracking capabilities, ensuring customers can monitor their item's progress as it moves across countries.

17. Answer: C) Through a thorough understanding of USPS services and asking the customer specific questions

Reason: By understanding the range of USPS services and inquiring about the customer's needs and preferences, clerks can make informed recommendations, ensuring the customer selects the most suitable mailing option.

18. Answer: A) Priority Mail

Reason: Priority Mail is typically recommended for packages that surpass the weight limits of First-Class Mail. It offers fast delivery and can handle a range of package sizes and weights.

19. Answer: B) For items that are heavy but fit inside the box, as the price is the same regardless of weight

Reason: USPS Flat Rate Boxes are priced based on the box's size, not its weight. Clerks might recommend this option to customers shipping heavier items that fit within the box's dimensions, offering potential cost savings.

20. Answer: A) Business Reply Mail

Reason: Business Reply Mail (BRM) allows businesses to provide pre-addressed envelopes or cards to their clients. The business pays the postage only for the returned pieces, making it an efficient and customer-friendly option.

21. Answer: C) Use cushioned mailers or bubble wrap, and mark the package as "Fragile."

Reason: For delicate items, it's vital to use protective packaging like cushioned mailers or bubble wrap to guard against damage during transit. Additionally, marking the package as "Fragile" alerts postal workers to handle the item carefully.

22. Answer: C) Suggest they verify the address before mailing

Reason: Accuracy in addressing is crucial for timely and successful mail delivery. If a customer is still determining an address, the best approach is to ask them to verify it before shipping to ensure it reaches the correct recipient.

23. Answer: C) Insurance and tracking for the mail piece

Reason: For valuable items, adding insurance provides financial protection if lost or damaged. Tracking allows the sender and recipient to monitor the mail piece's journey, offering peace of mind and ensuring timely delivery.

24. Answer: C) Priority Mail with return receipt

Reason: The "Return Receipt" service provides the sender with proof of delivery, including the recipient's signature upon receipt. This service is especially useful for important documents where delivery confirmation is essential.

25. Answer: C) It provides tracking information and assists in mail processing.

Reason: The Intelligent Mail Barcode is a barcode system used by the USPS to streamline and enhance mail processing. It provides tracking information for the sender and helps the postal service efficiently sort and route the mail.

26. Answer: C) Media Mail

Reason: Media Mail is a cost-effective USPS service designed to send educational materials, including books. While it might take longer than other services, its reduced rate makes it a popular choice for non-urgent media shipments.

27. Answer: B) Recommend another suitable USPS service

Reason: If a mail item doesn't meet the criteria for First-Class Mail due to its dimensions, the clerk should guide the customer toward another USPS service that can accommodate the item's size while still meeting the customer's needs.

28. Answer: B) By assisting one customer thoroughly before moving to the next

Reason: To ensure customer satisfaction and reduce errors, clerks must focus on one customer at a time and address all their needs before moving to the next patron.

29. Answer: D) Priority Mail Express

Reason: Priority Mail Express is the USPS's fastest service, guaranteeing overnight or next-day delivery for time-sensitive mail. It's the best recommendation for customers needing swift and guaranteed delivery times.

30. Answer: B) Use a postal scale to determine the exact postage

Reason: Postal scales provide accurate weight measurements for mail pieces, allowing clerks to assess the required postage. This ensures the mail is overpaid and paid and can be processed and delivered without issues.

31. Answer: B) To ensure accurate guidance and efficient service to customers

Reason: As front-line representatives of the USPS, clerks play a vital role in guiding and assisting customers. Keeping updated on the latest USPS policies and services ensures they provide accurate information and top-tier service, enhancing customer trust and satisfaction.

CONCLUSION

The realm of postal services is vast, dynamic, and ever-evolving. As we draw this comprehensive guide to a close, we've journeyed through the intricate facets of various USPS examinations, from maintenance and electronics (Exam 955) to the roles of mail carriers, handlers, and clerks (Exams 474, 475, and 477, respectively). Each chapter sheds light on the nuanced requirements, tasks, and considerations prospective postal workers should be well-versed in to excel in their chosen roles.

But why is such a guide essential, and what implications does it carry for those who aspire to join the postal force? At its core, the postal service is not just about moving letters or packages. It's a cornerstone of communication, ensuring that personal sentiments, legal documents, and essential goods reach from one hand to another, bridging distances and connecting lives. Each role within the USPS, whether front-facing or behind the scenes, contributes to this grand orchestration of logistics, customer service, and trust.

In this guide, we delved into the technicalities of various postal roles, underscoring the significance of each task. For instance, the maintenance and electronics sections highlighted the backbone of the USPS machinery, reminding us that the smooth operation relies heavily on the silent gears that turn in the background. On the other end of the spectrum, the customer service/clerk roles emphasized the importance of human interaction, communication, and problem-solving in maintaining the USPS's reputation as a reliable service.

Furthermore, the series of questions crafted for each examination served as a preparation tool and a reflection of the depth and breadth of knowledge required in the postal service. They underscored the need for precision, dedication, and a genuine understanding of the operation's technical and human sides.

In conclusion, the postal service, in all its manifestations, is a testament to human ingenuity, perseverance, and the relentless pursuit of connectivity. This book, in its essence, serves as both a beacon and a compass for those who wish to be part of this legacy. To all aspiring postal workers, may this guide be your trusted companion in your journey towards serving communities, bridging divides, and ensuring that every message finds its way home no matter the distance.

SPECIAL EXTRA CONTENT

Dear esteemed reader, If these final words are resonating with you, it signifies that you have successfully navigated through a path of personal and professional development, and we are privileged to have been part of your journey towards knowledge.

Your Insights Are Invaluable!
Your experiences, reflections, and feedback on the material you've just completed are crucial to us. We earnestly encourage you to share your thoughts about our book on Amazon. Whether a particular section struck a chord with you or the overall journey through the pages has broadened your understanding, your perspective is immensely important. By sharing your experiences, you help guide other learners and provide us, the authors, with the inspiration needed to refine our work and continue delivering impactful content.

Uncover Special EXTRA CONTENT Reserved Just for You!
In appreciation of your commitment, we've prepared exclusive additional content specifically for our readers. Here's what awaits you:

- **EXTRA 1: AUDIOBOOK (mp3 audio files)** from listening to whenever and wherever you want!: Complement your studies with an **included audiobook.** Whether you're on-the-move or just changing up your study approach, this guide meets you where you are.
- **EXTRA 2:** Unlock a comprehensive understanding of the U.S. Postal Service exams with our meticulously crafted set of **100 flashcards.** Tailored specifically for the aspirational postal exam candidate, this tool is available in a polished, **print-ready PDF** as well as an **interactive digital collection for the ANKI app**. Immerse yourself in crucial topics ranging *from mail handling protocols and safety measures to the intricacies of customer interactions and equipment maintenance.* Boost your Postal Service exam preparation with an edge – a standout feature exclusive to our guide!

You can track your progress and conveniently and interactively memorize the most important terms and concepts! Download to your device: **Anki APP or AnkiDroid,** or enter the web page and register free of charge. Then import the files we have given you as a gift and use the flashcards whenever and wherever you want to study and track your progress.

Straightforward Resources for Ongoing Enrichment
Below, you will find a distinctive QR CODE leading directly to your bonus content, ready for immediate download and exploration. There's no need for email subscriptions or personal detail disclosures; this is our direct gift to you, supporting your continued educational journey seamlessly.
Should you encounter any issues or have any questions regarding the downloadable material, please feel free to reach out to us at **booklovers.1001@gmail.com**

Sending warm regards and best wishes for your future endeavors.
With heartfelt thanks!
We look forward to your feedback!
Thank you!

Made in United States
Orlando, FL
05 August 2024

49945992R00059